FLORIDA TEST PREP

The Ultimate 3rd Grade Workbook for Mastering FAST Reading

Just 25 Enchanting Minutes a Day to Ace All B.E.S.T. ELA Standards

S. PRICE

TABLE OF CONTENTS

INTRODUCTION

Dear Parents, Guardians, and Educators,

Welcome to the FLORIDA TEST PREP: the Ultimate 3rd Grade Workbook for Mastering FAST Reading. This workbook emerges from our commitment to support the educational journey of children aged 8 to 9. Our goal extends beyond helping them excel in FAST reading tests; we aim to cultivate a deep-seated passion for reading in them. We firmly believe that without this foundational love for reading, the essence of learning diminishes.

We've designed this educational tool as a series of daily practice sessions that are light yet consistent, laying the groundwork for long-term growth in reading. Each session, lasting no more than 25 minutes, features engaging short texts followed by multiple-choice questions. This approach is intended to assess children's text comprehension, track their progress, and ensure that reading becomes an enjoyable lifelong habit.

Our focus is on specific ELA skills aligned with the B.E.S.T. standards to ensure effective preparation for the FAST exams, aimed at continuously improving children's understanding and critical analysis capabilities, thereby boosting their confidence in answering exam questions.

Additionally, the workbook includes supplemental resources such as clear self-assessment instructions and educational short stories about friendship, family, sharing, and teamwork. These are designed not only to provide further practice but also to inspire and motivate young readers on their path to growth.

Our primary purpose is to prepare children for tests and, more importantly, to help them develop reading skills that will serve them throughout their lives, far beyond the classroom walls. We encourage you to dive in, connect with the material, and enjoy the learning and development experience each session offers. Together, we can make a difference. Let's embark on this journey with enthusiasm!

*We are dedicated to crafting high-quality products and strive to ensure maximum customer satisfaction. We would be deeply grateful if you could contribute to our growth. Once you have finished reading the book, **your opinion would be immensely valuable to us**. Thank you from the bottom of our hearts!*

To claim your bonus, please proceed to:

Part 2: Solutions & Insights – BONUS

*This bonus includes **three comprehensive Reading Practice Tests** designed to prepare for the actual FAST Tests.*

PART

READING PRACTICE

LITERARY TEXTS

The Magical Treehouse

In a quaint little village, a mysterious treehouse was hidden deep within the woods between rolling hills and lush green forests. Legend had it that this treehouse possessed magical powers, granting wishes to those who dared to enter its enchanted realm. Every night, whispers of laughter and wonder echoed from its branches, like a friendly giant, the treehouse seemed to hug all the dreams of those who visited. Enticing curious souls from far and wide, it stood as a beacon of hope and adventure.

One sunny afternoon, three adventurous friends named Lily, Sam, and Max stumbled upon the mystical treehouse while exploring the forest. Excitement filled their hearts as they climbed the creaky wooden ladder and entered the cozy interior. To their amazement, the walls were adorned with shimmering crystals, and the air was filled with the scent of blooming flowers. They knew that their lives would never be the same again.

As the friends gazed around in awe, a soft voice spoke from the shadows, offering them a chance to make a wish. Each friend pondered their deepest desires, contemplating the power of the magical treehouse. With hopeful hearts, they whispered their wishes into the gentle breeze, trusting in the magic surrounding them. Little did they know, their wishes were about to set off a chain of extraordinary adventures beyond their wildest dreams.

And so, under the warm embrace of the stars, the three friends descended from the treehouse, carrying in their hearts the promise of endless adventures, certain that, whenever the desire for wonder called to them, that magical haven among the branches would be there waiting for them, ready to turn their dreams into reality.

Questions:

1. Read this sentence: "Like a friendly giant, the treehouse seemed to hug all the dreams of those who visited..."

What type of figurative language is used in this phrase?

A) Hyperbole

B) Metaphor

C) Personification

D) Simile

2. Why does the author use this type of figurative language?

A) To show how large the treehouse looks.

B) To illustrate the warm and protective welcome the treehouse offers to visitors.

C) To describe the physical structure of the treehouse.

D) To indicate how many visitors can enter the treehouse at once.

3. What greeted the friends as they entered the treehouse?

A) Shimmering crystals and blooming flowers.

B) A mysterious aura enveloping every corner with forgotten delicate scents.

C) A mosaic of soft lights dancing on the walls to the rhythm of the wind.

D) A subtle melody, almost imperceptible, that seemed to narrate ancient legends.

4. Select two sentences that support the author's depiction of the treehouse as a magical welcoming place for its visitors.

A) "Excitement filled their hearts as they climbed the creaky wooden ladder and entered the cozy interior."

B) "The walls were adorned with shimmering crystals, and the air was filled with the scent of blooming flowers."

C) "Every night, whispers of laughter and wonder echoed from its branches."

D) "A soft voice spoke from the shadows, offering them a chance to make a wish."

E) "They knew that their lives would never be the same again."

The Magical Bookstore

Nestled between the towering skyscrapers of the bustling city, there existed a quaint bookstore known as "Enchanted Pages." Despite its unassuming exterior, the shelves within held books that whispered secrets, tales of wonder, and adventures waiting to be embarked upon. Each book possessed its charm, and those who dared to enter the magical realm of "Enchanted Pages" often found themselves transported to far-off lands and fantastical worlds.

One ordinary afternoon, as the clock struck noon, a young girl named Emily stumbled upon the doorway to "Enchanted Pages" while wandering the city streets. Intrigued by the soft glow from within, she pushed open the creaky door and stepped into the cozy interior. Rows upon rows of books greeted her, their spines adorned with intricate designs and mysterious symbols. With anticipation tingling in her fingertips, Emily began exploring the enchanting world before her.

As Emily perused the shelves, her eyes fell upon a dusty tome tucked away in the corner of the store. Its cover, adorned with shimmering stars and swirling galaxies, seemed to beckon her closer. With trembling hands, she reached out and opened the book, only to be engulfed in a whirlwind of magic and wonder. Before she knew it, Emily stood amid an ancient forest surrounded by towering trees and mystical creatures. Little did she realize her journey through the pages of the magical bookstore had only just begun?

Questions:

1. Read this sentence: "The shelves within held books that whispered secrets, tales of wonder, and adventures waiting to be embarked upon..."

Which type of figurative language is used in this phrase?

A) Hyperbole

B) Metaphor

C) Personification

D) Simile

2. Why does the author use this type of figurative language?

A) To illustrate the vast quantity of books in the bookstore.

B) To suggest that the bookstore is noisy.

C) To convey the magical, inviting atmosphere of the bookstore and the potential for adventure that the books offer.

D) To indicate the physical layout of the bookstore.

3. How does Emily's experience change in "The Magical Bookstore"?

A) At first, she is curious but overwhelmed at the end..

B) At first, she's curious and excited, then she ends up totally amazed.

C) At first, she is bored but excited at the end.

D) At first, she is lost but feels at home at the end.

4. How does the text develop the theme that curiosity can lead to magical adventures?

A) Emily walks past the bookstore without noticing its magic, deciding it looks too ordinary.

B) Emily decides to explore the bookstore further after initially finding it uninteresting.

C) Emily is drawn into the bookstore by a soft glow and discovers a book that transports her to another world.

D) Emily buys a book on impulse without looking inside, missing the magical journey it could offer.

The Secret Circus

Hidden away in a secret grove deep within the woods, there existed a circus unlike any other. Known as the "Whispering Grove Circus," it was said to appear only to those who truly believed in the world's magic. With its colorful tents and mesmerizing performances, the circus offered a glimpse into a realm of wonder and enchantment that few were privileged to witness.

One moonlit night, as the stars twinkled overhead and the forest echoed with the songs of nocturnal creatures, a young boy named Alex stumbled upon the entrance to the secret circus. Drawn by laughter and the flickering glow of torches, he pushed aside the dense foliage and stepped into the hidden clearing where the circus awaited. With wide eyes and a heart full of excitement, Alex joined the audience to witness the extraordinary spectacle unfolding.

Alex marveled at their acrobatics, magic, and illusion feats as the performers approached the stage. From daring tightrope walks to breathtaking fire dances, each act held him spellbound, filling him with a sense of wonder and awe. As the night wore on, he was swept away on a whirlwind adventure, dancing with clowns, befriending exotic animals, and discovering the true magic within the heart of the secret circus.

Questions:

1. Read the sentence: "Alex marveled at their acrobatics, magic, and illusion feats." In this context, what does "marveled" mean?

A) Became confused

B) Was amazed

C) Felt scared

D) remained indifferent

2. How does the author convey what makes the secret circus special?

A) By detailing the exotic animals' roles in the shows.

B) By describing every colorful tent and its contents.

C) By explaining why people are drawn to the hidden circus in the forest.

D) By illustrating how performers interact with the audience at the circus.

3. What drew Alex to the secret circus?

A) The smell of popcorn and cotton candy.

B) The sound of laughter and the glow of torches.

C) The promise of exotic animals and daring acrobatics.

D) The opportunity to meet new friends.

4. Which two statements should be part of a summary of "The Secret Circus"?

A) Alex accidentally finds the entrance to the hidden circus on a moonlit evening.

B) Alex enjoys refreshments handed out by the circus crew.

C) Alex is captivated by the sound of laughter and the soft light of torches.

D) Alex watches the performers get ready before the show kicks off.

E) Alex experiences incredible performances and makes friends with unusual animals.

The Magic Paintbrush

A young artist named Mei lived in a quaint village at the foot of mist-covered mountains. Despite her humble surroundings, Mei possessed a talent that seemed to transcend the ordinary - the ability to bring her paintings to life with a single stroke of her brush. With colors as vibrant as the sunrise and imagination as boundless as the sky, Mei's artwork captured the hearts of all who beheld its enchanting beauty.

One serene afternoon, while exploring the depths of the ancient forest that bordered her village, Mei stumbled upon a hidden glade bathed in golden sunlight. In the center of the glade stood a gnarled oak tree, its branches stretching towards the heavens like outstretched arms. Drawn by an irresistible urge, Mei approached the tree and reached out to touch its rough bark, unaware of the dormant magic within its ancient roots.

As Mei's fingers brushed against the oak tree's trunk, a spark of energy surged through her veins, infusing her with a newfound sense of purpose. With trembling hands, she retrieved her paintbrush from her pouch and began to sketch upon her mind's canvas, allowing the forest's magic to guide her hand. With each stroke, the world around her transformed as flowers bloomed at her feet and birds sang melodies of joy from the treetops.

Questions:

1. How does the author convey what makes Mei's paintbrush special in "The Magic Paintbrush"?

A) By illustrating the transformation of Mei's surroundings as she paints.

B) By detailing the different colors Mei uses in her artwork.

C) By explaining the process Mei follows to create her paintings.

D) By showcasing the reactions of the village people to Mei's art.

2. Read this sentence: "In the center of the glade stood a gnarled oak tree, its branches stretching towards the heavens like outstretched arms." Which type of figurative language is used in this phrase?

A) Hyperbole.

B) Metaphor.

C) Personification.

D) Simile.

3. Why does the author use this type of figurative language in "The Magic Paintbrush"?

A) To create a vivid image of the tree and glade, making readers feel as if they are there with Mei.

B) To suggest that the tree is about to change shape right before Mei's eyes.

C) To indicate that Mei has the power to transform the tree with her paintbrush.

D) To foreshadow the transformation Mei will experience through her art.

4. What transformation occurred as Mei began to paint in the glade?

A) The sky darkened, and a storm began.

B) Flowers bloomed, and birds sang melodies.

C) The trees withered, and the air grew cold.

D) The glade disappeared, leaving Mei lost.

The Mysterious Locket

In the attic of a very old house, among lots of forgotten and dusty things, there was a small and pretty locket with detailed designs and a mysterious feel to it. A long time had passed since anyone knew what happened to the person who last owned it, and there were many secrets and questions left behind. Even though it might not look like much, this locket was the key to solving a very old mystery.

On a stormy night, with loud thunder and lightning lighting up the sky, a young girl named Lily found this dusty locket while she was exploring the attic of the house where her family has lived for many generations. She felt as if something was pulling her towards it, so she picked it up and immediately felt a rush of energy. Wanting to know more, Lily decided to find out everything about this strange locket and what happened to the person who had it before.

As Lily looked more into the locket's secrets, she found old writings, strange symbols, and old photos hidden in the house. Each thing she found out brought her closer to solving the mysteries about the locket and how it was connected to her family's history. Finally, when she figured out the last piece of the puzzle, Lily was ready to discover a truth that her family had not known for a very long time.

Questions:

1. How does the author develop the central idea that looking into the locket's past can help us understand more about Lily's family history?

A) By talking about how the locket's secrets are like those of other old family treasures.

B) By showing how the locket and its mysteries are linked to Lily's family story.

C) By telling us the locket is more mysterious than other things found in the house.

D) By explaining why the locket's past is important to know more about Lily's family tree.

2. In the story, what does "aura" mean when it says the locket has "intricate engravings and a mysterious aura"?

A) Color

B) Shape

C) A special feeling or atmosphere

D) Size

3. Why did Lily want to find out all the secrets of the locket?

A) She was curious about its mysterious feeling.

B) She wanted to learn more about her family's past.

C) Stories of adventure and mystery made her excited.

D) She thought about selling it for a lot of money.

4. In the story, what does "ancestors" mean when it says Lily was "ready to find out a truth that her ancestors hadn't known for generations"?

A) People who will come after

B) Friends of the family

C) Family members from a long time ago

D) Neighbors

The Mystery of Whispering Woods

Deep within the heart of Whispering Woods, where ancient trees whispered secrets and shadows danced beneath the moon's gentle glow, a mystery awaited. Legends spoke of a hidden treasure concealed within the forest's depths, guarded by mystical creatures and enchanted barriers. Despite the dangers that lurked within, brave adventurers dared to venture into the whispering woods in search of fortune and glory.

One fateful evening, as twilight descended upon the land and the air crackled with magic, a young wanderer named Aria stumbled upon the entrance to Whispering Woods. Drawn by tales of adventure and the promise of treasure, she hesitated only briefly before plunging into the shadows of the ancient forest. With a map clutched tightly in her hand and determination burning in her heart, Aria embarked on a journey that would change her life forever.

As Aria navigated the twisting paths and tangled undergrowth of Whispering Woods, she encountered challenges that tested her courage and resolve. From riddles whispered by mischievous spirits to trials of strength and cunning, each obstacle brought her one step closer to unraveling the mystery of the forest. And when, at last, she stood before the hidden chamber where the treasure lay, Aria realized that the greatest reward was not the gold and jewels that gleamed within but the lessons she had learned and the friends she had made along the way.

Questions:

1. Read this sentence from the story: "where ancient trees whispered secrets and shadows danced beneath the moon's gentle glow." Which type of figurative language is used in this phrase?

A) Hyperbole

B) Metaphor

C) Personification

D) Simile

2. Why does the author use this type of figurative language in the story?

A) To create a vivid and magical setting that captivates the reader.

B) To explain the scientific properties of trees and shadows.

C) To provide a detailed history of Whispering Woods.

D) To outline the geography of the forest.

3. What motivated Aria to venture into Whispering Woods?

A) Tales of adventure and the promise of treasure

B) A desire to explore ancient ruins

C) A need to escape her mundane life

D) A dream of meeting mystical creatures

4. What did Aria realize as she stood before the hidden chamber in the forest?

A) The importance of friendship and lessons learned

B) The need to guard the treasure from others

C) The value of the gold and jewels within

D) The desire to explore more forests for treasures

The Lost Explorer

In the heart of the dense jungle, where sunlight struggled to pierce the thick canopy of trees and the air hummed with the calls of exotic creatures, there lay the ruins of an ancient civilization waiting to be rediscovered. Known as the Lost City of Eldorado, it was said to hold untold riches and ancient artifacts long forgotten by time. Despite countless expeditions searching for its elusive treasures, the city remained hidden, shrouded in mystery and intrigue.

One fateful day, as the sun hung high in the sky and the jungle teemed with life, a daring explorer named Diego set out to uncover the secrets of the Lost City of Eldorado. Driven by a thirst for adventure and a desire to unravel the mysteries of the past, he plunged deep into the heart of the jungle, following ancient maps and cryptic clues in search of his elusive prize.

As Diego journeyed more profoundly into the jungle, he encountered obstacles that tested his courage and determination. From treacherous ravines to swarms of biting insects, each challenge brought him one step closer to unlocking the secrets of Eldorado. And when, at last, he stood before the crumbling ruins of the lost city, Diego realized that the greatest treasure was not the gold and jewels that glittered within but the knowledge that he had uncovered and the adventures that lay ahead.

Questions:

1. How does Diego's behavior change in the text?

A) He becomes more fearful as he faces the jungle's dangers.

B) He grows more determined with each obstacle he encounters.

C) He decides to give up his search for the Lost City of Eldorado.

D) He starts doubting the existence of the Lost City of Eldorado.

2. Select which sentence shows why Diego's feelings changed?

A) "Driven by a thirst for adventure and a desire to unravel the mysteries of the past, he plunged deep into the heart of the jungle."

B) "From treacherous ravines to swarms of biting insects, each challenge brought him one step closer to unlocking the secrets of Eldorado."

C) "Despite countless expeditions searching for its elusive treasures, the city remained hidden, shrouded in mystery and intrigue."

D) "And when, at last, he stood before the crumbling ruins of the lost city, Diego realized that the greatest treasure was not the gold and jewels."

3. What is the purpose of Diego's exploration in the narrative?

A) To find and bring back gold and jewels.

B) To prove that the Lost City of Eldorado does not exist.

C) To uncover the knowledge and adventures that lay ahead.

D) To escape the monotony of his daily life.

4. How does the author develop the central idea that adventure and knowledge are greater treasures than gold and jewels?

A) By detailing the wealth and opulence of the Lost City of Eldorado.

B) By highlighting Diego's initial desire for material wealth.

C) By describing the obstacles Diego overcomes in his quest.

D) By concluding with Diego's realization of what he truly values.

The Magical Forest Picnic

In the heart of a lush forest, where sunlight danced through the canopy, and the air was alive with the chatter of woodland creatures, there lay a secret clearing known only to a select few. This enchanted glade was perfect for a picnic with its soft grass and sparkling stream. And so, one bright morning, a group of friends named Mia, Jake, and Lily set out with baskets of goodies and hearts full of excitement for a day of adventure in the magical forest.

As they skipped the winding path, the friends stumbled upon a patch of colorful mushrooms, their caps dotted with dewdrops that sparkled like diamonds in the sunlight. Intrigued by the sight, Mia reached out to touch one, and in an instant, they were transported to a world of wonder and whimsy. Trees stretched towards the sky like towering giants, and flowers bloomed in hues of every color imaginable. With wide eyes and laughter on their lips, Mia, Jake, and Lily set off to explore the magical forest picnic.

As they wandered deeper into the forest, the friends encountered fantastical creatures from storybooks - talking animals, mischievous fairies, and even a gentle unicorn grazing in a sunlit meadow. Together, they feasted on berries sweeter than honey and sandwiches filled with laughter and friendship. As the sun began to dip below the horizon, casting a golden glow over the treetops, Mia, Jake, and Lily knew they would cherish this day in the magical forest forever.

Questions:

1. What was special about the secret clearing in the forest?

A) It was home to a group of friendly animals.

B) It was enchanted and known only to a few.

C) It was filled with dangerous creatures.

D) It was a popular spot for picnics.

2. How does the story show that going on a search can lead to exciting new discoveries? Choose two answers:

A) By showing Mia, Jake, and Lily finding a hidden treasure map.

B) By describing how the friends find a secret clearing for a picnic.

C) By telling about the magical creatures they meet on their adventure.

D) By explaining how they get lost and find their way home.

3. What does "excitement" mean in the situation where it says "...and hearts full of excitement..." as Mia, Jake, and Lily start their adventure?

A) They were feeling sleepy.

B) They were feeling bored.

C) They were feeling happy and eager.

D) They were feeling confused.

4. What type of figurative language is used in the phrase "...that sparkled like diamonds in the sunlight"?

A) Metaphor

B) Simile

C) Personification

D) Hyperbole

The Mystery of Lost Puppy

A young girl named Emily lived in the cozy neighborhood of Maplewood, where colorful houses lined the streets, and laughter filled the air. Emily had always dreamed of having a furry companion to call her own, and one sunny morning, her wish came true when she stumbled upon a lost puppy wandering the streets. With big, soulful eyes and a wagging tail, the puppy captured Emily's heart, and she knew she had to help reunite him with his family.

Determined to solve the mystery of the lost puppy's identity, Emily set out on a quest through the neighborhood, knocking on doors and asking if anyone recognized the adorable canine. Along the way, she encountered friendly neighbors who offered encouragement and clues to aid in her search. With each new lead, Emily grew more determined to unravel the mystery and bring the lost puppy back home where he belonged.

After hours of searching, Emily's efforts finally paid off when she stumbled upon a flyer posted on a lamppost with a picture of the lost puppy and a phone number to call. With trembling hands, Emily dialed the number and was overjoyed to hear the relieved voice of the puppy's owner on the other end of the line. With a grateful heart, Emily returned the lost puppy to his family, knowing she had made a difference in their lives.

Questions:

1. Read the sentence "With trembling hands, Emily dialed the number and was overjoyed to hear the relieved voice of the puppy's owner on the other end of the line."

What does "trembling" mean in this context?

A) Moving quickly

B) Shaking because of feelings, like being nervous or excited

C) Holding tightly

D) Being very strong

2. Choose the text that best describes the story:

A) Emily is going to adopt a new puppy from the animal shelter.

B) Emily is going on a trip to find a magical forest.

C) Emily finds a lost puppy and decides to help reunite it with its family.

D) Emily is organizing a neighborhood pet show.

3. How does the story tell us what happened to Emily and the puppy in order, from start to finish?

A) By talking about how Emily felt before and after she found the puppy.

B) By listing the reasons Emily wanted a puppy.

C) By telling us each thing that happened, one after the other, until the puppy got home.

D) By telling us how the puppy changed the neighborhood.

The Adventures of Captain Courage

A young boy named Timmy lived in the bustling port town of Seaside Cove, where seagulls soared overhead, and ships sailed into the horizon. Timmy dreamt of becoming a brave pirate captain, sailing the seven seas for treasure and adventure. Inspired by tales of swashbuckling heroes, Timmy donned a makeshift pirate hat and set out on imaginary voyages aboard his trusty toy ship, the Sea Serpent.

One stormy night, as Timmy watched from his bedroom window, a lightning bolt illuminated the dark sky, revealing a shadowy figure standing on the shore. Intrigued, Timmy grabbed his toy telescope and peered through the glass, only to gasp in amazement as the figure transformed into a rugged pirate captain. With a hearty laugh and a twinkle in his eye, the captain introduced himself as Captain Courage and invited Timmy to join him on a daring adventure across the high seas.

Timmy leaped aboard the Sea Serpent without hesitation, ready to embark on the adventure of a lifetime. Together, he and Captain Courage braved treacherous storms, outwitted cunning sea monsters, and discovered hidden treasures beyond their wildest dreams. Along the way, Timmy learned valuable lessons about bravery, friendship, and the power of imagination. And as they sailed back into Seaside Cove under the light of a full moon, Timmy knew that he would cherish the memories of his adventures with Captain Courage forever.

Questions:

1. Which type of figurative language is used in the description "seagulls soared overhead, and ships sailed into the horizon"?

A) Hyperbole

B) Metaphor

C) Personification

D) Simile

2. Why does the author use this type of figurative language in describing the setting of Seaside Cove?

A) To show the danger of the sea

B) To make it seem calm

C) To highlight its beauty and activity

D) To show it's cut off from everything else

3. How does Timmy's view on adventures change by the end of his journey with Captain Courage?

A) He realizes adventures are better in stories.

B) He learns that real adventures are as exciting as he imagined.

C) He decides he prefers everyday life to adventures.

D) He wishes to go back in time before the adventure

4. What lessons did Timmy learn during his adventures with Captain Courage?

A) Lessons about bravery, friendship, and the power of imagination.

B) Lessons about cooking and baking.

C) Lessons about math and science.

D) Lessons about sportsmanship and teamwork.

The Lost Treasure of Pirate Cove

In the coastal town of Seabreeze Bay, nestled between rolling hills and the sparkling sea, there are whispered tales of a long-lost treasure buried deep within the cliffs of Pirate Cove. Generations of adventurers had sought the fabled riches, but none had returned with more than stories of peril and mystery. Among the intrigued locals was Lily, a spirited young girl passionate about exploration. Determined to unravel the secrets of Pirate Cove, Lily embarked on a daring quest that would test her courage and cunning.

As Lily ventured into the treacherous cliffs of Pirate Cove, she encountered numerous obstacles, from hidden traps to cunning puzzles left behind by the pirates of old. Undeterred by the challenges, Lily pressed on, fueled by the thrill of the unknown and the hope of uncovering the legendary treasure. Along the way, she forged unlikely friendships with fellow adventurers and learned valuable lessons about perseverance and teamwork.

After days of tireless exploration, Lily finally stumbled upon the entrance to a hidden cavern deep within the cliffs. With bated breath, she ventured into the darkness, her heart racing with anticipation. And there, illuminated by the soft glow of her lantern, Lily discovered the long-lost treasure of Pirate Cove - a chest overflowing with glittering jewels and ancient artifacts. Though the journey had been fraught with danger, Lily emerged victorious from the depths of Pirate Cove, her courage and determination rewarded with riches beyond her wildest dreams.

Questions:

1. How does the story summarize its plot and main theme?

A) Going on an adventure helps you learn about yourself; it's all about being brave.

B) Solving a mystery with friends; it's about working together.

C) Traveling through history; it's about learning from old stories.

D) Getting through tough times; it's about not giving up.

2. How does Lily change throughout the story?

A) Learns to overcome fears, demonstrating courage.

B) Discovers a new passion, indicating growth.

C) Makes a new friend, highlighting the value of friendship.

D) Doesn't change much, maintaining her initial traits.

3. What does Lily learn during her adventure in Pirate Cove?

A) Lessons about the importance of greed.

B) Lessons about the dangers of exploration.

C) Lessons about perseverance and teamwork.

D) Lessons about staying away from danger.

4. Which sentences should be included in a summary of the passage?

A) Lily always dreamed of finding the lost treasure of Pirate Cove.

B) Lily meets a wise old adventurer who gives her a map.

C) Lily discovers the treasure in a hidden cavern deep within the cliffs.

D) Lily decides to give up her quest after encountering the first obstacle.

The Mysterious Case of Missing Book

In the bustling halls of Riverview Elementary School, excitement filled the air as students eagerly awaited the grand unveiling of the school's newest library addition - a rare and precious book rumored to hold the key to unlocking magical powers. Among the eager students was Emily, a bookworm with a penchant for adventure. But when the time came to reveal the book, it was nowhere to be found. Thus began the mysterious case of the missing book, and Emily was determined to unravel the puzzle and restore the magic to Riverview Elementary.

Armed with her trusty magnifying glass and keen detective skills, Emily searched every nook and cranny of the school in pursuit of clues. Along the way, she enlisted the help of her classmates, each bringing their unique talents to the investigation. Together, they uncovered a trail of breadcrumbs - from cryptic messages scribbled in library books to mysterious footprints leading to the school's attic. The mystery deepened with each discovery, and Emily's determination to solve the case grew stronger.

After days of tireless sleuthing, Emily and her classmates finally cracked the case of the missing book. It had been hidden away by a mischievous ghost who had taken a liking to the enchanting tale within its pages. With the book safely returned to its rightful place, the magic was restored to Riverview Elementary, and Emily emerged as a hero among her peers. But the thrill of the investigation had sparked something within her - a love for adventure and a newfound confidence in her ability to solve any mystery that came her way.

Questions:

1. How does Emily's behavior change in the text?

A) At first, she is curious but becomes determined by the end.

B) At first, she's timid but becomes confident at the end.

C) At first, she is skeptical but feels accomplished at the end.

D) At first, she is indifferent but becomes passionate by the end.

2. Select which sentence shows why Emily changed her feelings:

A) Initially, she prefers to read alone, but then she enjoys collaborating with classmates.

B) At first, she doubts her detective skills, but then she successfully leads the investigation.

C) Initially, she is afraid of the school's attic, but then she braves it to find the book.

D) Initially, she is just interested in reading, but then she discovers a love for adventure.

3. How is Emily's perspective different from her classmates'?

A) Emily is focused on solving the mystery, while her classmates are more interested in the book's magic.

B) Emily thinks about the adventure, but her classmates think about the consequences.

C) Emily is driven by curiosity, while her classmates are motivated by the reward.

D) Emily values teamwork, while her classmates prioritize individual recognition.

4. Which type of figurative language is used when describing Emily's quest as "Armed with her trusty magnifying glass and keen detective skills"?

A) Hyperbole

B) Metaphor

C) Simile

D) Personification

INFORMATIONAL TEXTS

The Amazing World of Dolphins

Dolphins are intriguing species that inhabit waters all over the globe. They are classified as cetaceans, together with whales and porpoises. Dolphins' intellect is one of their most impressive characteristics. They are considered very gregarious creatures, sometimes migrating in groups called pods. Dolphins interact with one another via a range of noises and gestures, demonstrating intricate social behaviors that scientists continue to study and appreciate.

Dolphins have unique adaptations that enable them to flourish in the oceanic environment. Their sleek bodies are ideal for swimming, with muscular tails propelling them through the water at high speeds. Dolphins have a superb sense of echolocation, which they utilize to travel and find prey. This skill allows them to detect food even in dark or muddy waters, making them very effective hunters.

Despite their intellect and flexibility, dolphins suffer various challenges in their natural environment. Dolphins face multiple issues, including pollution, habitat deterioration, and being entangled in fishing gear. Conservation initiatives are ongoing to preserve these beautiful species for future generations.

Questions:

1. Identify the text structure used in the passage about dolphins.

A) Compare-contrast

B) Sequential

C) Problem-solution

D) Descriptive

2. Match the cause to its effect:

Cause: Dolphins' ability to use echolocation.

Effects:

A) They can communicate over long distances.

B) They can find food in dark or muddy waters.

C) They suffer from habitat destruction.

D) They are able to fly in formation.

3. What is one remarkable adaptation that dolphins have?

A) They can breathe underwater

B) They have wings for flying

C) They have a strong sense of echolocation

D) They have fur to keep them warm in the water

4. Select the primary concept that unifies all aspects of the text.

A) The importance of conserving dolphin habitats

B) The unique social behaviors of dolphins

C) Dolphins are intelligent and adaptive creatures facing various environmental threats

D) The process of echolocation in dolphins

The Marvelous World of Bees

Bees are beautiful creatures that play an essential part in our environment. They are well-known for their tireless efforts as pollinators, assisting plants in reproducing by transporting pollen from one blossom to another. Bees live in well-organized colonies, each consisting of a queen bee, worker bees, and male drones. The queen bee lays eggs, while worker bees gather nectar and pollen, construct and maintain the hive, and look after the young bees.

One of the most intriguing elements of bees is their intricate communication system. Bees interact with one another via a variety of methods, including complicated dances known as "waggle dances." These dances provide crucial information regarding the location of food supplies, water, and suitable nesting areas. By witnessing these dances, bees can send exact directives to their colony members, guaranteeing optimal foraging and hive care.

Despite their diminutive size, bees encounter several obstacles in today's environment. Bee populations across the globe are in danger from habitat loss, pesticide usage, climate change, and illness. The loss of bee populations is a cause for significant worry since it impacts not only the bees but also agriculture and biodiversity. Safeguarding bees and their habitats is critical for preserving ecosystem health and providing human food security.

Questions:

1. Match cause to its effect:

Cause: Bees performing "waggle dances."

Effects:

A) Bees are able to communicate precise locations of food and resources.

B) The queen bee lays more eggs.

C) Bees produce more honey.

D) The hive becomes overcrowded.

2. Compare the roles within a bee colony based on the passage.

A) Worker bees and queen bees both lay eggs.

B) Male drones and worker bees gather nectar and pollen.

C) Worker bees maintain the hive, whereas the queen bee's primary role is to lay eggs.

D) All bees in the colony perform the waggle dance to communicate.

3. What is the main purpose of the passage?

A) To explain how bees produce honey.

B) To persuade readers to support bee conservation efforts.

C) To describe the lives and challenges of bees.

D) To instruct readers on how to care for bees.

4. What are some challenges faced by bees mentioned in the passage?

A) Habitat loss, pesticide use, and climate change

B) Overpopulation and deforestation

C) Desertification and hunting

D) None of the above

The Amazing World of Rainforests

Rainforests are rich and colorful ecosystems that exist in tropical locations all over the globe. They are home to various plant and animal species, with millions more remaining. Rainforests regulate the Earth's temperature by absorbing CO_2 and creating oxygen via photosynthesis. These biodiverse environments also provide numerous essential resources, such as medicine, food, and materials for daily items.

One of the most intriguing elements of rainforests is their distinct structure and strata. Rainforests consist of many strata, including the emergent layer, canopy layer, understory layer, and forest floor. Each layer creates a unique environment for diverse plants and animals, with varying degrees of light, temperature, and humidity. This vertical structure facilitates a complex web of species interactions, contributing to the richness and complexity of rainforest ecosystems.

Despite their value, rainforests face tremendous dangers from human activity. Deforestation, agriculture, logging, and mining are the primary drivers of rainforest damage, resulting in habitat loss and fragmentation. This damage endangers the existence of innumerable plant and animal species while also contributing to global climate change and biodiversity loss. Conservation activities are essential for safeguarding and conserving these rich ecosystems for future generations.

Questions:

1. Select the sentence where the author states opinions:

A) "Rainforests are rich and colorful ecosystems that exist in tropical locations all over the globe."

B) "These biodiverse environments also provide numerous essential resources, such as medicine, food, and materials for daily items."

C) "Deforestation, agriculture, logging, and mining are the primary drivers of rainforest damage."

D) "Conservation activities are essential for safeguarding and conserving these rich ecosystems for future generations."

2. Match cause to its Effects:

Cause: Human activity such as deforestation, agriculture, logging, and mining.

Effects:

A) Increase in rainforest biodiversity.

B) Enhancement of global climate change and biodiversity loss.

C) Improvement in the Earth's temperature regulation.

D) Expansion of rainforest areas.

3. What does "biodiversity" mean?

A) The different kinds of weather places can have.

B) The number of trees found in a forest.

C) All the different types of living things like plants, animals, tiny bugs you can barely see, and mushrooms.

D) How plants use sunlight to make food.

4. Select the primary concept that unifies all aspects of the text.

A) Rainforests give us lots of stuff we use every day.

B) Rainforests have layers like a cake, and each layer is home to different animals and plants.

C) Rainforests are in big trouble because of things people are doing, and we need to help protect them.

D) How rainforests make their food from sunlight.

Exploring the Solar System

The solar system is a significant and intriguing location, including the sun, eight planets, moons, asteroids, comets, and other cosmic objects. The sun, a giant star, sits at the solar system's core, providing light, heat, and energy to the planets that circle it. Our solar system has eight planets: Mercury, Venus, Earth, Mars, Jupiter, Saturn, Uranus, and Neptune. Each planet has distinct properties, such as size, composition, and atmosphere, making them fascinating study subjects for scientists and astronomers.

The solar system has several moons that circle the planets. Moons vary in size and form, with some more significant than others. For example, Earth's moon is quite giant relative to the planet it circles, while other moons are tiny and irregularly shaped. Moons play an essential role in creating the ecosystems of the planets they orbit, affecting tides, weather patterns, and possibly the potential of life.

For decades, scientists and space organizations have aimed to explore the solar system. Robotic spacecraft, such as NASA's Voyager and Mars rovers, have offered vital insights into faraway planets and their moons. Human space travel has also helped us comprehend the solar system, with astronauts landing on the moon and performing research on space stations. Continued investigation and study are required to reveal the solar system's secrets and advance our understanding of the cosmos.

Questions:

1. How does the size and shape of moons compare to the planets they orbit?

A) All moons are larger than the planets they orbit.

B) Moons are uniformly shaped and similar in size.

C) Some moons are quite large relative to their planets, while others are tiny and irregularly shaped.

D) Each moon is exactly half the size of its planet.

2. What does "cosmic objects" mean in the context of the solar system?

A) Only planets and stars

B) Any natural object outside the Earth's atmosphere, including planets, moons, asteroids, and comets

C) Artificial satellites orbiting Earth

D) The sun and the moon only

3. What is the main purpose of the passage?

A) To detail the history of space travel

B) To argue for increased funding for space exploration

C) To introduce the components of the solar system and highlight the importance of exploration

D) To describe the process of photosynthesis in plants on Earth

4. What role do moons play in the solar system?

A) Influencing tides and weather patterns

B) Providing light and heat

C) Orbiting around stars

D) None of the above

The Amazing World of Dinosaurs

Dinosaurs were magnificent animals that inhabited the Earth millions of years ago. They appear in various forms and sizes, from giant, long-necked sauropods to terrifying meat-eating tyrannosaurs. Dinosaurs existed throughout the Mesozoic Era, sometimes known as the "Age of Dinosaurs." They controlled the globe for nearly 160 million years before abruptly vanishing, leaving remains and clues for scientists to solve their riddles.

Dinosaurs are remarkable due to their enormous variety. They lived in various environments, from lush forests to deserts, and adapted to distinct lifestyles. Some dinosaurs were herbivores, eating plants and trees, while others were carnivores, hunting and preying on other creatures. Dinosaurs also possessed distinguishing characteristics such as armor plating, horns, spikes, and even feathers, which enabled them to survive and prosper in their habitats.

Scientists have made astounding discoveries regarding dinosaurs using fossil evidence and study. They have identified hundreds of dinosaur species and studied their behavior, anatomy, and evolutionary history. Scientists are constantly learning more about dinosaurs' existence by researching fossils and comparing them to living species, such as how they moved, communicated, and interacted with their surroundings. Dinosaurs continue to captivate the imaginations of people of all ages, instilling curiosity and wonder about the ancient world they lived in.

Questions:

1. Match cause to its Effects:

Cause: Dinosaurs' adaptations to their environments.

Effects:

A) They dominated the globe for nearly 160 million years.

B) They could only live in lush forests.

C) All dinosaurs became carnivores.

D) They developed features like armor plating, horns, spikes, and feathers.

2. How did herbivorous and carnivorous dinosaurs differ in their lifestyles?

A) Both relied on the same food sources.

B) Herbivores ate plants and trees, while carnivores hunted other creatures.

C) Carnivores had feathers, while herbivores had armor plating.

D) Both lived exclusively in deserts.

3. What do scientists study to learn about dinosaurs?

A) Fossils

B) Meteorites

C) Seashells

D) Tree rings

4. What is the main purpose of the passage?

A) To argue that dinosaurs never existed and are a myth.

B) To detail the process of fossilization in dinosaurs.

C) To introduce the diversity and significance of dinosaurs and the insights gained from studying them.

D) To provide a step-by-step guide on becoming a paleontologist.

The Marvels of Coral Reefs

Coral reefs are like underwater cities full of colors and life. They are made up of tiny sea creatures called coral polyps. These little creatures work together to build their home from a substance called calcium carbonate, which becomes the coral reef. People often call coral reefs "rainforests of the sea" because, just like rainforests, they are home to lots of different kinds of life.

Coral reefs are very important for the ocean and for people too. They provide a home for many sea animals and plants, protect beaches from waves, and even help people by providing food and a place to enjoy activities like snorkeling and diving.

However, coral reefs are in trouble because of things like pollution, overfishing, and the water getting warmer and more acidic due to climate change. This can cause a problem called coral bleaching, where corals lose their colors and get sick. It's important to take care of coral reefs so they can stay healthy and keep being wonderful parts of the ocean.

Questions:

1. Match cause to its Effects:

Cause: Increasing water temperatures and ocean acidity.

Effects:

A) Coral reefs grow faster.

B) Loads more fish come to live there.

C) Coral bleaching happens, and the corals can get sick and might not survive.

D) There are more fun things to do like snorkeling and diving.

2. Why coral reefs are called the "rainforests of the sea"?

A) Because they are made of rainwater.

B) Because they are colorful.

C) Because they have lots of different animals and plants living there.

D) Because they're found in places where it's really warm and rains a lot.

3. What roles do coral reefs play in marine ecosystems?

A) They give homes to lots of sea animals.

B) They act like big walls that protect the beaches.

C) They help people by giving them food and places to have fun.

D) All of the above.

4. What is the main purpose of the passage?

A) To explain how coral reefs are formed.

B) To talk about fun water activities related to coral reefs.

C) To tell us why coral reefs are super important and why we need to look after them.

D) To compare coral reefs to other marine ecosystems.

Exploring Volcanoes: Nature's Spectacular Phenomenon

Volcanoes are like nature's fireworks - they can explode with lava, ash, and gases from underneath Earth's surface. You can find them everywhere in the world, from small hills to giant mountains. Volcanic eruptions are mighty, creating beautiful and sometimes scary landscapes. But even though they can be destructive, volcanoes play a big part in making new land and helping lots of different plants and animals survive.

Volcanic eruptions happen because of tectonic plates - big pieces of Earth's crust - moving and sometimes crashing into each other underneath the ground. This can make magma come up and cause a volcano to erupt. There are many types of volcanoes, like shield volcanoes, stratovolcanoes, and cinder cone volcanoes, each with its own way of erupting and kind of lava. Some places, like the Pacific Ring of Fire, have lots of active volcanoes because of the way the Earth's plates crash there.

Scientists who study volcanoes are called volcanologists. They use special tools to watch volcanoes to see when they might erupt and learn more about how they work. This helps keep people safe and teaches us more about our planet.

Questions:

1. Match cause to its Effects:

Cause: The movement of tectonic plates.

Effects

A) The world gets warmer.

B) Volcanoes start forming and erupting.

C) New ocean currents are made.

D) Animals start moving to different places.

2. Which sentence best reflects the author's opinion on the importance of volcanoes?

A) "Volcanoes are amazing parts of Earth, made from exploding rock, ash, and gases from below."

B) "Even though they can be scary, volcanoes help change the Earth and are home to many living things."

C) "The reason volcanoes erupt is because of how Earth's plates move and hit each other."

D) "There are lots of volcano types, like shields and cones, each erupting in its own special way."

3. Select the primary concept that unifies all aspects of the text.

A) The dangerous nature of volcanoes.

B) The beauty of volcanic landscapes.

C) Learning about and watching volcanoes to better understand our planet and keep people safe.

D) The history of volcanoes and their eruptions over time.

4. Why is studying volcanoes important?

A) To really get how Earth works and changes.

B) To figure out when volcanoes might erupt and what dangers they bring.

C) To help scientists explore and learn more about nature.

D) For all these reasons: understanding Earth, predicting dangers, and exploring new things.

The Lifecycle of Butterflies

Butterflies are exciting creatures with bright colors and delicate wings. They undergo a spectacular change known as metamorphosis, which has four stages: egg, larva (caterpillar), pupa (chrysalis), and mature butterfly. A butterfly's life cycle starts when a female lays eggs on the leaves of a host plant. These eggs hatch into tiny caterpillars that feast on the leaves and develop quickly.

Molting is when a caterpillar loses its skin several times as it develops. The caterpillar eventually grows to its full size and creates a protective shell known as a chrysalis or pupa. The caterpillar undergoes a spectacular change within the chrysalis, breaking down its bodily components and reorganizing them into butterfly-like structures. This procedure might take many days or weeks, depending on the species.

The mature butterfly emerges from the chrysalis, unfolds its wings, and pumps fluids into them, causing them to enlarge and harden. When the butterfly's wings are completely formed, it makes its maiden flight in search of honey and a partner. The mature butterfly's principal purpose is reproducing and completing its life cycle. After mating, the female butterfly lays eggs, which restarts the cycle. The life cycle of a butterfly is a stunning illustration of nature's splendor and the significance of adaptability for survival.

Questions:

1. How is the caterpillar stage different from the chrysalis stage in a butterfly's life?

A) In the caterpillar stage, it moves around and eats a lot of leaves. In the chrysalis stage, it doesn't move and changes into a butterfly.

B) The caterpillar eats leaves in both the caterpillar and chrysalis stages.

C) The caterpillar can fly in both stages.

D) There's no difference; they're just different names for the same thing.

2. Select the primary concept that unifies all aspects of the text.

A) The beauty of butterflies.

B) The process of metamorphosis in butterflies.

C) The diet of caterpillars.

D) How butterflies fly.

3. What does "metamorphosis" mean in the context of butterflies?

A) The process of laying eggs.

B) The change from a caterpillar to a butterfly.

C) The ability to fly.

D) Eating leaves to grow.

4. What is the primary goal of an adult butterfly?

A) To eat leaves

B) To find a mate and reproduce

C) To build a nest

D) To sleep in a cocoon

The Importance of Recycling

Recycling is like turning trash into treasure so it doesn't end up making the planet dirty or taking up space in dumps. It's super important for keeping our natural treasures safe, cutting down on pollution, and helping fight climate change. When we recycle things like paper, plastic, glass, and metal, we use less energy, make less air pollution, and keep animals' homes safe. Recycling helps us use stuff in a smart way, making less trash.

One big plus of recycling is that it helps keep the planet clean and uses less stuff. For example, recycling paper means we don't need to cut down as many trees, and it uses less water and power. Also, turning old aluminum cans back into new ones uses a lot less energy and makes the air cleaner than making aluminum from new materials. Recycling means less trash goes to places like dumps and burners, which can make the air and water yucky.

Recycling is not just good for Earth; it's also good for people. It creates jobs for folks who collect, sort, and turn trash into new things. It also helps towns save money by reducing the cost of dealing with trash and making money from selling recycled stuff. By supporting recycling and learning about why it's so important, we all can help keep our planet healthy and happy for a long time.

Questions:

1. How is using old paper different from making new paper from trees?

A) Both use the same amount of trees and water.

B) Using old paper saves trees and energy, but making new paper uses more.

C) Making new paper saves more trees.

D) Neither affects the environment.

2. Question: What is the text structure of "The Importance of Recycling" passage?

A) Compare-contrast

B) Sequential

C) Problem-solution

D) Descriptive

3. What is the main purpose of the passage?

Aa) To persuade readers to avoid recycling.

B) To inform readers about the importance and benefits of recycling.

C) To compare different methods of waste disposal.

D) To narrate the history of recycling practices.

4. Select the sentence where the author states opinions:

A) "Recycling transforms waste into reusable items so they do not wind up in landfills or pollute the environment."

B) "Recycling paper, for example, saves trees, water, and energy."

C) "We can work together to safeguard the earth and create a sustainable future for future generations."

D) "Recycling generates employment in waste management, manufacturing, and recycling facilities."

The Marvelous World of Penguins

Penguins are super cool birds that love the cold, especially in places like Antarctica and other spots in the Southern Hemisphere. They stand out with their black-and-white colors, funny walk, and amazing swimming skills. Penguins are built to handle the cold with their thick feathers for warmth, sleek bodies for speedy swimming, and waterproof feathers to stay dry. These awesome birds hunt for fish, squid, and krill in the sea, zooming through the water using their wings like flippers.

Even though they can't fly, penguins are graceful swimmers. Their wings turned into flippers help them move fast underwater, almost like flying through the sea. They can dive really deep to find food, with some types going down as much as 500 meters! Penguins have great eyesight in and out of the water, which helps them spot food and find their way around their water world. Penguins also like to stick together, living in big groups where they find partners, take care of their babies, and talk to each other with different sounds and actions.

Penguins are perfect for living in super cold places but face a lot of problems, like climate change, too much fishing, dirtiness, and losing their homes. Warmer weather and melting ice make it hard for penguins to find food and places to live. Too much fishing takes away their food, and dirty stuff like oil spills can hurt penguins and mess up where they live. Saving penguins and their chilly homes means making safe ocean spots and cutting down on air pollution.

Questions:

1. Compare the swimming ability of penguins to their flying ability.

A) Penguins can both swim in water and fly in the air with equal skill.

B) Penguins are awesome swimmers with their flipper-like wings underwater, but they can't fly.

C) Penguins are better at flying than swimming.

D) Penguins prefer to walk rather than swim or fly.

2. Select the primary concept that unifies all aspects of the text:

A) Penguins' diet.

B) How penguins are built to live in cold places.

C) The threats facing penguins.

D) Penguins as social animals.

3. What are some threats to penguins mentioned in the passage?

A) Hurricanes, earthquakes, and tsunamis.

B) Desertification, deforestation, and volcanic eruptions.

C) Warmer weather, too much fishing, dirty places, and losing their homes.

D) None of the above.

4. What is the text structure of the passage about penguins?

A) Compare-contrast.

B) Sequential.

C) Problem-solution.

D) Descriptive.

Amazing Animal Adaptations

Animals have remarkable skills to adapt to their surroundings. The chameleon, a reptile famed for its ability to change color to fit in with its environment, is an excellent example. This adaption enables the chameleon to dodge predators and sneak up on prey. Another remarkable example is the polar bear, which uses massive layers of fat and a dense fur coat to stay warm in the frigid Arctic conditions. These adaptations enable polar bears to flourish in one of the toughest habitats on the planet.

Animals have both physical and behavioral adaptations that help them survive. Meerkats, for example, are tiny animals in African deserts that live in gangs and take turns standing guard to keep predators at bay. This action protects the group from harm as they seek for food. Similarly, migratory birds such as the Arctic tern fly hundreds of kilometers yearly to locate food and ideal nesting locations, demonstrating their exceptional navigation abilities.

Some animals have evolved novel methods to gather food. Anteaters, for example, have a long, sticky tongue to gather ants and termites, their principal food sources. With its long neck and prehensile tongue, the giraffe can reach foliage high in trees that other animals cannot. These specific feeding adaptations enable animals to utilize various food sources and flourish in a wide range of settings worldwide.

Questions:

1. How is the way chameleons avoid predators different from how meerkats do it?

A) Chameleons change color, while meerkats take turns standing guard.

B) Both chameleons and meerkats fly to escape predators.

C) Chameleons and meerkats both use speed to run away.

D) There is no difference; both animals use the same method.

2. Select the primary concept:

A) Animals like to move around.

B) Animals have special ways to live in their homes.

C) All animals eat the same food.

D) Animals talk to each other the same way.

3. How is the story about amazing animal adaptations told?

A) By comparing different animals.

B) Step by step, from one animal to the next.

C) By showing a problem animal's face and how they solve it.

D) Describing how different animals live and survive.

4. Match Cause to Its Effects:

Cause: Animals adapting to their environments.

Effects:

A) Chameleons blend into their surroundings.

B) Polar bears stay warm in cold places.

C) Meerkats watch out for dangers together.

D) All of the above.

Incredible Inventions

Inventions have totally changed how we live and see the world around us. A super cool invention is the light bulb, made by Thomas Edison in 1879. Before we had light bulbs, people had to use candles, oil lamps, and gas lamps to see in the dark, which wasn't very bright and could be pretty risky. The light bulb made it way easier and safer to light up places like homes and offices everywhere.

Then there was Alexander Graham Bell who came up with the telephone in 1876, and it was a huge deal. Thanks to the telephone, people could talk to each other from far away in real time, which was a big step for the world of communication. Before the phone, if you wanted to send a message far away, you had to write a letter or use a telegraph, which took a lot longer. The telephone made it super quick to reach out to someone, no matter how far they were.

Lately, new tech stuff like smartphones have shown up and changed everything again. A smartphone is like having a phone, computer, camera, and more all in your pocket. Smartphones have changed how we talk to each other, have fun, and find information, making it easy to stay connected and know what's going on all the time. As we come up with more cool tech, we're going to see even more amazing stuff that we can't even imagine yet

Questions:

1. How did the light bulb invention by Thomas Edison compare to earlier forms of lighting?

A) It wasn't brighter but was safer to use.

B) It gave off more light and was safer and more trusty than candles or oil lamps.

C) It wasn't really brighter or safer than the old lights.

D) It was brighter but could be more risky.

2. What's the story mostly about?

A) How electricity came to be.

B) How we got better at talking over distances.

C) How some super smart ideas changed the way we do everyday stuff.

D) When famous people who invent things were born.

3. Which sentence best shows the impact of these inventions?

A) "Inventions can be interesting to learn about."

B) "These inventions have revolutionized the way we live and interact."

C) "Many people have made inventions."

D) "Inventions are always happening."

4. Select the sentence where the author states opinions:

A) When they say Thomas Edison made the light bulb in 1879.

B) Saying the telephone let people chat instantly over long distances.

C) Talking about how smartphones changed the way we chat, have fun, and look stuff up.

D) Saying that as we invent more stuff, we're going to see even cooler things.

Marvels of the Ocean

The ocean is home to various intriguing species, ranging from tiny plankton to massive whales. The sea turtle is one of the most fascinating aquatic species. Sea turtles have been swimming in the waters for millions of years and are recognized by their unique shells and flippers. These prehistoric reptiles migrate hundreds of kilometers across the ocean to eat and nest. Sea turtles play an essential role in the health of marine ecosystems by regulating jellyfish and other prey populations.

The octopus is another intriguing creature of the water. Octopuses are clever organisms with sophisticated nerve systems that can solve problems and learn from their surroundings. They utilize their eight arms to swim smoothly through the water and catch prey like crabs and shellfish. Octopuses are masters of camouflage, changing colors and textures to fit in with their environment and escape predators. Their extraordinary talents make them one of the most fascinating organisms in the water.

The water also supports an astonishing array of fish species, from small guppies to gigantic sharks. Fish occur in various forms, sizes, and colors, each tailored to its niche in the aquatic environment. Some fish, like clownfish, have symbiotic relationships with other animals, including sea anemones. Others, such as anglerfish, have developed unique hunting methods, attracting prey in the ocean's dark depths using bioluminescent lures.

Questions:

1. How does the octopus's method of avoiding predators compare to the sea turtle's?

A) Both change color to escape predators.

B) The octopus uses camouflage, while the sea turtle relies on its shell for protection.

C) Both use speed as their main defense.

D) Sea turtles use camouflage, and octopuses rely on their shells.

2. What main idea connects everything in the passage?

A) How sea creatures manage to stay safe.

B) The cool ways sea creatures live and survive in the ocean.

C) What sea creatures like to eat.

D) The process of discovering new sea creatures.

3. Select the sentence where the author states opinions:

A) "Sea turtles have been around for millions of years."

B) "Fish come in many shapes and sizes."

C) "Their cool tricks make them some of the most awesome animals in the ocean."

D) "Octopuses have eight arms."

4. What is the main purpose of the passage?

A) To convince us to save the ocean.

B) To teach us about the different creatures living in the ocean.

C) To describe a day in the life of a sea turtle.

D) To explain how fish breathe underwater.

MIXED TEXTS

Exploring the Animal Kingdom

The animal realm teems with magnificent animals, each with its qualities and habits. The chameleon is a fascinating species noted for its ability to change color and fit in with its environment. Chameleons employ camouflage to avoid predators and sneak up on prey. Furthermore, their large tongues enable them to grab insects with lightning-fast accuracy. Observing chameleons in their natural environment gives insight into their extraordinary adaptations.

Another fascinating species is the octopus, which has eight limbs and extraordinary intellect. Octopuses are masters of disguise, able to change their skin texture and color to resemble rocks or seaweed. They use their arms to investigate and handle items, solve puzzles, and open jars relatively quickly. The octopus' capacity to adapt to varied situations and perform hard tasks demonstrates the intellect and inventiveness of these aquatic animals.

The third astonishing species is the monarch butterfly, noted for its tremendous migration. Monarchs migrate hundreds of miles from Canada to Mexico to avoid the harsh winter weather. They handle challenges such as weather patterns and predators, depending on instinct and environmental signals for guidance. Witnessing the enormous migration of monarch butterflies is a magnificent display that demonstrates the tiny insects' endurance and fortitude.

Questions:

1. Match cause to its Effects:

Cause: Chameleon's ability to change color.

Effects:

A) It can avoid predators more effectively.

B) It captures prey without being noticed.

C) It can fly from one tree to another.

D) It sings to communicate with other chameleons.

2. How do chameleons and octopuses avoid predators?

A) Both can fly short distances to escape.

B) Each changes its body color, but octopuses can also change their skin texture to look like rocks or seaweed.

C) Chameleons use their large tongues, while octopuses solve puzzles.

D) Both primarily use their speed to escape predators.

3. What does "camouflage" mean in the context of the animal kingdom?

A) The ability to run very fast

B) The skill to sing beautifully

C) The skill to blend into the environment to avoid predators or sneak up on prey

D) The process of migrating long distances

4. What is the main idea of the passage?

A) The importance of speed in the animal kingdom

B) The unique ways animals adjust to their environments

C) The diet of various animal species

D) The sleeping patterns of animals

Uncovering Mysteries

Long ago, people built amazing things and came up with cool ideas that we're still trying to figure out today. The ancient Egyptians are famous for their huge pyramids and the Sphinx. These big old statues and buildings from thousands of years ago make us wonder how people back then lived and what they believed in. By looking at pharaohs' tombs and figuring out hieroglyphics, we can learn a lot about what life was like in ancient Egypt.

The Maya people from a long time ago in what's now Mexico, Guatemala, and Belize were also super smart. They built incredible cities and temples hidden in the jungle. They were really good at math and watching the stars, which helped them make really accurate calendars and track stars and planets. By studying old Maya stuff, we can learn about their way of life.

The ancient Greeks were all about thinking, art, and creating a way for people to have a say in their government, which has had a big influence on how we live today. From the big temples in Athens to the stories about gods and heroes, what we know from ancient Greece still affects our world. By reading Greek stories, myths, and checking out historical spots, we get to know more about where a lot of our culture comes from.

Questions:

1. How is the Greek perspective different from the Maya?

A) Greeks focused on philosophy and democracy, while Maya focused on mathematics and astronomy.

B) Greeks built in stone, while Maya built in the forests.

C) Greeks were not interested in building monumental structures.

D) There is no difference; both civilizations had similar interests.

2. Identify text structure:

A) Compare-contrast

B) Sequential

C) Problem-solution

D) Descriptive

3. Choose the option that best summarizes the passage:

A) The process of building the pyramids.

B) The contributions of ancient civilizations to modern culture.

C) The daily activities of ancient Greeks.

D) The wars between the Egyptians and the Maya.

4. Match cause to its Effects:

Cause: Studying ancient civilizations.

Effects:

A) Understanding how they built monumental structures.

B) Gaining insights into their culture, religion, and daily life.

C) Learning about their advancements in mathematics and astronomy.

D) All of the above.

The Mystery of Lost Key

In a lovely village hidden amid rolling hills and lush woods, a group of friends set off on an exciting quest to unravel the mystery of the missing key. Emma, Jack, and Mia discovered an ancient map in Emma's attic. With its enigmatic patterns and fading writing, the map made them assume that a buried treasure awaited discovery. Determined to solve the mystery, the companions embarked on an exciting and intriguing voyage.

Their journey led them through twisting trails and intriguing tunnels as they followed the map's hints. They met unforeseen obstacles and weird monsters hiding in the shadows along the journey. Despite their anxieties, the buddies used collaboration and tenacity to overcome difficulties and continue their search for the misplaced key. With each step, they got closer to discovering the mysteries buried in the old map.

After hours of hunting, the buddies eventually found a secret room deep beneath the jungle. They discovered a rusting box with a forgotten lock and moss-covered surface inside. With bated breath, they inserted the key they had worked so hard to locate. A light lit the room as the lock snapped open, exposing a treasure beyond their wildest expectations. With hearts full of excitement and amazement, Emma, Jack, and Mia recognized that the treasure was not the wealth they had discovered but the friendship connections formed throughout their voyage.

Questions:

1. Identify text structure:

A) Compare-contrast

B) Sequential

C) Problem-solution

D) Descriptive

2. Why does the author describe the monsters as "weird"?

A) To show the friends were scared

B) To make the story more exciting

C) To explain why the monsters were hiding

D) To show the monsters were actually friendly

3. Select the sentence where the author states opinions:

A) "They discovered a rusting box with a forgotten lock and moss-covered surface inside."

B) "With hearts full of excitement and amazement..."

C) "The treasure was not the wealth they had discovered but the friendship connections formed."

D) "They met unforeseen obstacles and weird monsters hiding in the shadows."

4. What is the main purpose of the passage?

A) To teach about ancient maps.

B) To narrate an adventure that strengthens friendship.

C) To provide historical information about hidden treasures.

D) To instruct on how to read maps.

The Magical Island Adventure

Once upon a time, a magical island was cloaked in fog and mythology. Few people knew about this island, rumored to have treasures beyond comprehension. One beautiful day, a group of interested youngsters found a map indicating the secret island's location. Excited by the potential of adventure, they set off on a tiny boat, eager to discover the island's secrets.

As they reached the island, the youngsters were astounded by its lush flora and cliffs. They parked their boat on the sandy beach, exploring the island's deep woods and twisting paths. They saw unique wildlife along the route, such as colorful birds, lively monkeys, and brilliant fireflies. Each step moved them closer to discovering the island's mysteries.

After hours of exploring, the youngsters discovered a secret cave deep inside the woods. They found ancient relics and luminous crystals that lit up the cavern walls. As they looked in astonishment, they knew the island had magical abilities beyond their wildest imaginations. With hearts full of excitement and amazement, the youngsters pledged to protect the island's mysteries and treasure the memories of their remarkable experiences forever.

Questions:

1. Which type of figurative language is used in the following sentence?

"The Island was cloaked in fog and mythology."

A) Hyperbole, meaning the island was very foggy.

B) Metaphor, meaning the island was mysterious and full of ancient stories.

C) Personification, giving the island human qualities.

D) Simile, comparing the island to a storybook.

2. How does the text develop the theme that searching can lead to new discoveries?

A) By showing the youngsters discovering a secret cave.

B) By describing the island's magical abilities.

C) By detailing the wildlife they see.

D) All of the above.

3. How does the magical abilities of the island different from the usual places the youngsters have known?

A) The island has ancient relics and luminous crystals, unlike their usual playgrounds.

B) The island is just like their local park.

C) The island has no wildlife, making it less interesting.

D) The island and their hometown have the same magical properties.

4. Select the primary concept that unifies all aspects of the text:

A) The importance of following a map accurately.

B) Magical creatures and where to find them.

C) The adventure and discoveries leading to a deeper appreciation of friendship.

D) Learning about ancient relics and their uses.

The Secret of Haunted House

In a peaceful neighborhood, a home was covered in mystery and gossip. The inhabitants dubbed it the "Haunted House," thinking ghosts and spirits haunted it. One daring group of friends, desperate to discover the truth, investigated the mansion on a fateful Halloween night. Armed with torches and bravery, they entered, oblivious of the mysteries that awaited them.

The buddies felt shivers down their spines as they reached the dimly illuminated entryway. Cobwebs hung from the ceiling, and dust covered the furnishings, creating an unsettling atmosphere. Undeterred, they continued, cautiously inspecting each room and passageway. Strange sounds resonated through the hallways, and shadows flickered across the walls, deepening their discomfort.

They uncovered a secret stairway to the basement deep inside the property. They sank with apprehension into the darkness below, their hearts racing with expectation. They were surprised to discover a bounty of antique relics and hidden valuables rather than ghosts. Among the antiques was a journal belonging to the property's previous owner, which revealed the terrible story of lost love and betrayal that had plagued the place for years.

Questions:

1. What is the main idea of the passage?

A) The house is actually haunted by ghosts.

B) The house is full of dangerous traps.

C) The friends find a treasure instead of ghosts.

D) The house is completely empty.

2. Which type of figurative language is used when describing the "shivers down their spines"?

A) Hyperbole

B) Metaphor

C) Personification

D) Simile

3. Why does the author the figurative language "shivers down their spines"?

A) To make the story sound more factual and scientific.

B) To add humor and make the readers laugh.

C) To increase the feeling of fear and suspense in the story.

D) To describe the weather inside the house.

4. How does the text develop the theme that bravery leads to new discoveries?

A) The friends run away as soon as they hear strange sounds.

B) The friends decide to explore the house despite their fears.

C) The friends call for help when they find the secret stairway.

D) The friends ignore the antique relics and leave the house.

The Mystery of Hidden Treasure

Once upon a time, a fascinating tradition circulated among the residents about a secret treasure buried deep beneath the forest in the tiny hamlet of Willowbrook. The tale talked of a courageous explorer who had buried the wealth years before, leaving a trail of clues for those who were brave enough to pursue it. Determined to discover the truth, a group of youthful explorers journey to unravel the mystery of the buried wealth.

As the youthful adventurers traversed the deep jungle, they found several hurdles and barriers. They traced clues carved into old trees, solved riddles engraved into aged stones, and braved perilous passages guarded by clever traps. Along the journey, they learned the importance of tenacity, cooperation, and critical thinking as they collaborated to uncover the forest's mysteries and locate the treasure.

After many hardships and tribulations, the youthful explorers reached the forest's heart, finding a secret cave under a gushing waterfall. They discovered the long-lost treasure inside the cave: a chest brimming with gold money, sparkling diamonds, and rare antiques. Overwhelmed with delight and excitement, the young explorers celebrated their success, knowing that their tenacity and dedication had led them to discover the greatest treasure — the ties of friendship and the rush of adventure.

Questions:

1. Which text best describes the story?

A) A group of friends finds a treasure in their garden.

B) Young explorers solve riddles to find a hidden treasure.

C) An old sage tells treasure stories to the village children.

D) A pirate hides his treasure on a deserted island.

2. How do the protagonists' behaviors change in the text?

A) Become more selfish.

B) Lose interest in the adventure.

C) Learn the value of friendship and adventure.

D) Become less courageous.

3. Select the sentence that shows why the protagonists' feelings changed:

A) "At the start of the adventure, they were excited about finding the treasure."

B) "After solving the last riddle, they realized that the real wealth was the friendship they had built."

C) "The constant rain made the journey less enjoyable each day."

D) "The maps were confusing and difficult to follow, but this did not stop the young explorers."

4. What does "tenacity" mean in the way it's used in the text?

A) The ability to solve difficult puzzles.

B) The skill of navigating a forest.

C) The determination to overcome challenges and not give up.

D) The enthusiasm for finding treasures.

The Mystery of the Missing Artifacts

An unusual case perplexed citizens in Brightsville, a busy metropolis. Several expensive relics vanished from the local museum overnight, leaving everyone needing clarification. Detective Max, known for his acute eye and smart intellect, accepted the task of solving the case. Detective Max used his trusty magnifying glass to analyze every trace, from footprints to fingerprints, in his quest for the elusive criminal.

Detective Max dug further into the case and discovered a breadcrumbs trail leading to the city's mysterious underground tunnel system. Detective Max entered the dark tunnels like a ship navigating through a stormy sea, with confidence in his heart and resolve in his gaze, daring to face the unknown. Along the way, he met various difficulties, including concealed traps and sophisticated decoys put up by the astute burglar to dissuade any pursuit.

After an exciting pursuit through the labyrinthine tunnels, Detective Max apprehended the criminal in a concealed room deep down. To his amazement, the burglar was the museum's curator, Mr. Jenkins, who was motivated by avarice to take the treasures for personal benefit. Detective Max became triumphant after recovering the treasures and apprehending the offender, restoring peace and justice to Brightsville.

Questions:

1. Which sentence uses a metaphor or a simile?

A) "An unusual case perplexed citizens in Brightsville, a busy metropolis."

B) "Detective Max used his trusty magnifying glass to analyze every trace."

C) "Detective Max entered the dark tunnels like a ship navigating through a stormy sea, with confidence in his heart and resolve in his gaze."

D) "After an exciting pursuit through the labyrinthine tunnels, Detective Max apprehended the criminal."

2. What is the meaning of the figurative language in the chosen sentence?

A) Detective Max is literally sailing a ship.

B) The tunnels are filled with water like the sea.

C) Detective Max's journey through the tunnels is as challenging and uncertain as navigating a stormy sea.

D) The criminal is hiding in the sea.

3. What does "avarice" mean in the way it's used in the text?

A) Bravery

B) Cleverness

C) Greed

D) Sadness

4. Which two sentences should be included in a summary of the passage?

A) "Detective Max used his trusty magnifying glass to analyze every trace."

B) "To his amazement, the burglar was the museum's curator, Mr. Jenkins."

C) "Detective Max entered the dark tunnels with confidence in his heart and resolve in his gaze."

D) "Detective Max became triumphant after recovering the treasures and apprehending the offender."

The Secret Garden

Most inhabitants are not aware of a hidden garden in the center of Greenfield village. This fascinating garden, hidden behind a thick curtain of ivy and tall oak trees, contains secrets to be uncovered. One bright day, Lucy, a curious girl with a taste for adventure, accidentally finds the garden's entrance while exploring the woods. Lucy is intrigued by the murmurs of its existence and ventures through the ivy-covered gate into a world of wonder.

As Lucy progresses into the garden, she comes across various vivid flowers, each with its own story. The buzzing of bees and birds chirping fills the air, producing a symphony of noises that resonate through the woods. Lucy sees a little stone fountain among the blossoms, its waters glistening in the sunshine. Mesmerized by its beauty, she touches the cold surface, feeling a calm flood over her.

As the day ends, Lucy regretfully says goodbye to the hidden garden, knowing she will return soon. With astonishment and excitement, she retraces her travels through the woods, ready to tell her friends and family about her find. Little does she realize that the hidden garden is more than simply beautiful; it is the key to releasing her imagination and starting on endless adventures.

Questions:

1. What does "mesmerized" mean in the way it's used in the text?

A) Confused

B) Frightened

C) Captivated

D) Lost

2. Which sentence uses a metaphor or a simile?

A) "Lucy, curious and adventurous, accidentally finds the entrance to the garden while exploring the woods."

B) "The buzzing of bees and birds chirping fills the air, producing a symphony of noises."

C) "Lucy sees a little stone fountain among the blossoms, its waters glistening in the sunshine."

D) "As the day ends, Lucy knows she will soon return to visit the hidden garden."

3. What is the meaning of the figurative language in the chosen sentence?

A) The bees and birds literally form an orchestra.

B) The garden is actually a concert hall.

C) The sounds of nature in the garden are as harmonious and beautiful as a symphony.

D) Lucy can play musical instruments.

4. How does the author develop his purpose of explaining what's special about the garden?

A) By listing all the plants in the garden.

B) Through Lucy's reactions and the vivid descriptions of her experiences.

C) By explaining the history of each flower.

D) Using scientific names for all the garden's creatures.

Exploring the Mysterious Cave

A fascinating cave was deep in the forest in a little village amid rolling hills. According to legend, the cave contained a treasure guarded by a fierce dragon. Despite the townspeople's warnings, a bold group of friends went on an expedition to discover the cave's mysteries.

As they moved further into the forest, the companions met various challenges, including dangerous pathways and strange animals. Undaunted, they continued, driven by curiosity and a feeling of adventure. They eventually reached the cave's entrance, cloaked in darkness and mystery.

With shaky hands and racing hearts, the pals entered the cave, their candles throwing spooky shadows over the walls. They discovered old engravings and secret rooms as they continued investigating, each revealing a piece of the cave's mysterious history. However, as they dug further, they found they were not alone, and the real struggle lay ahead.

Questions:

1. What does "undaunted" mean in the way it's used in the text?

A) Scared

B) Careless

C) Unafraid

D) Confused

2. Which two sentences should be included in a summary of the passage?

A) "According to legend, the cave contained a treasure guarded by a fierce dragon."

B) "A bold group of friends went on an expedition to discover the cave's mysteries."

C) "With shaky hands and racing hearts, the pals entered the cave."

D) "They discovered old engravings and secret rooms as they continued investigating."

3. How does the author develop his purpose of explaining what's special about the cave?

A) By describing the physical appearance of the cave.

B) Through the friends' daring journey and discoveries inside the cave.

C) Listing the types of treasures found in the cave.

D) Explaining the history of the village.

4. How does the protagonists' behavior change in the text?

A) They become more frightened as they enter the cave.

B) They become more curious and determined as they face challenges.

C) They decide to give up and go back home.

D) They become less interested in the cave's mysteries.

The Library Adventure

Once upon a time, in a little village set amid rolling hills, there existed a magnificent library known as the Enchanted Bookshelf. This library was no ordinary structure; it was rumored to house volumes that could transport readers to mystical worlds and faraway locations. One bright day, a group of eager youngsters went to discover the Enchanted Bookshelf for themselves.

As they entered the library, they were met with towering shelves loaded with volumes of every shape, size, and color. The air was thick with the aroma of ancient paper and ink, and the quiet sound of pages turning resonated down the hall. Excited by the possibilities, the youngsters divided off to seek their adventure between the pages of a book.

One group of youngsters entered the world of a dusty old book found in a neglected nook of the library. As they read over its yellowed pages, they were caught up in a whirl of enchantment and found themselves amid a mythical woodland. Trees murmured secrets in the breeze, and weird animals hurried among the shadows, sending the youngsters on an exciting adventure to discover the mysteries of the magical forest.

Meanwhile, another set of youngsters found a book that claimed to transport them across time. They read its pages with anxiety and excitement, being taken back to ancient Egypt to witness the building of the magnificent pyramids and the beauty of the pharaoh's court. Each successive chapter took them closer to solving the riddles of the past and discovering the secrets of a forgotten civilization.

Questions:

1. Which sentence uses a metaphor or a simile?

A) "Volumes of every shape, size, and color filled the shelves."

B) "Trees murmured secrets in the breeze."

C) "The youngsters entered the library with great enthusiasm."

D) "Candles dimly lit the interior of the library."

2. What does the figurative language communicate about the magical forest?

A) The trees were actually talking to the children.

B) The forest was very windy.

C) The magical forest was alive with mysteries and hidden stories.

D) It was difficult to move through the forest because of the trees.

3. How does the behavior of the protagonists change throughout "The Library Adventure"?

A) They become scared and decide to leave the library.

B) They lose interest in the books and the magic of the library.

C) Their excitement and curiosity grow as they explore the magical worlds.

D) They become tired and fall asleep in the library.

4. Which two sentences should be included in a summary of the passage?

A) "This library was no ordinary structure; it was rumored to house volumes that could transport readers to mystical worlds and faraway locations."

B) "One group of youngsters entered a dusty old book in a neglected library nook."

C) "They read its pages with anxiety and excitement, being taken back to ancient Egypt."

D) "Each successive chapter took them closer to solving the riddles of the past and discovering the secrets of a forgotten civilization."

PART

2

SOLUTIONS & INSIGHTS – BONUS

Upon purchasing the book, you are entitled to a bonus. To receive your bonus, please scan the QR code.

ANSWERS TO LITERARY TEXTS

The Magical Treehouse

1. What type of figurative language is used in this phrase?

Answer: D) Simile

Explanation: A simile compares two things using 'like' or 'as'. Here, the treehouse is compared to a giant, showing it's welcoming and big

2. Why does the author use this type of figurative language?

Answer: B)

Explanation: The simile makes us feel the treehouse is warm and safe, like a giant giving a friendly hug.

3. How does the author develop the theme of the magic within the treehouse?

Answer: A) By describing how shimmering crystals and blooming flowers welcome the friends.

Explanation: The description of shimmering crystals and blooming flowers immediately introduces the visitors to the enchanting and welcoming interior of the treehouse, setting the stage for their magical adventure.

4. Select two sentences that support the author's depiction of the treehouse as a magical welcoming place for its visitors.

Answer: B) "The walls were adorned with shimmering crystals, and the air was filled with the scent of blooming flowers".

Answer: C) "Every night, whispers of laughter and wonder echoed from its branches."

Explanation: Shiny crystals, sweet-smelling flowers, and happy laughter show that the treehouse is a magical and welcoming place, inviting everyone to step into a world full of magic and warmth.

The Magical Bookstore

1. Which type of figurative language is used in this phrase?

Answer: C) Personification

Explanation: Personification gives human traits to things. Here, books seem to whisper, making them feel alive.

2. Why does the author use this type of figurative language?

Answer: C) To convey the magical, inviting atmosphere of the bookstore and the potential for adventure that the books offer.

Explanation: This makes the bookstore feel magical, as if books can talk and take us on adventures.

3. How does Emily's experience change in "The Magical Bookstore"?

Answer: B) At first, she's curious and excited, then she ends up totally amazed.

Explanation: Emily goes from cautious to amaze as she finds magical adventures in the books.

4. How does the text develop the theme that curiosity can lead to magical adventures?

Answer: C) Emily is drawn into the bookstore by a soft glow and discovers a book that transports her to another world.

Explanation: Emily's curiosity about the glowing bookstore leads her to magical discoveries, showing curiosity is good.

The Secret Circus

1. In this context, what does "marveled" mean?

Answer: B) Was amazed

Explanation: Marveled means Alex was amazed by the circus's magic and fun.

2. How does the author convey what makes the secret circus special?

Answer: C) By explaining why people are drawn to the hidden circus in the forest.

Explanation: The circus is special because it's magical and only for those who believe in such magic.

3. What drew Alex to the secret circus?

Answer: B) The sound of laughter and the glow of torches.

Explanation: Laughter and glowing torches drew Alex to discover the circus.

4. Which two statements should be part of a summary of "The Secret Circus"?

Answer: A) Alex accidentally finds the entrance to the hidden circus on a moonlit evening.

Answer: C) Alex is captivated by the sound of laughter and the soft light of torches.

Explanation: These choices succinctly capture crucial moments of the narrative, highlighting Alex's discovery of the circus and what initially draws him into its enchanting world, setting the stage for his magical adventure.

The Magic Paintbrush

1. How does the author convey what makes Mei's paintbrush special in "The Magic Paintbrush"?

Answer: A) By illustrating the transformation of Mei's surroundings as she paints.

Explanation: The story highlights the paintbrush's unique ability to bring Mei's art to life, changing her surroundings and showing a special connection with magic.

2. Which type of figurative language is used in this phrase?

Answer: D) Simile

Explanation: The correct answer is simile because the phrase uses "like" to compare the tree's branches to arms, showing how they reach up high, which is a typical way similes illustrate similarities between different things.

3. Why does the author use this type of figurative language in "The Magic Paintbrush"?

Answer: A) To create a vivid image of the tree and glade, making readers feel as if they are there with Mei.

Explanation: The author describes the tree and the clearing in a special way so that when you read it, you can almost see and feel the beautiful place just like Mei does. It's like using words to paint a picture in your mind, so you feel like you're standing right there in the magical glade with her.

4. What transformation occurred as Mei began to paint in the glade?

Answer: B) Flowers bloomed, and birds sang melodies.

Explanation: The paragraph describes the world around Mei beginning to transform as she painted in the glade, with flowers blooming at her feet and birds singing melodies of joy, indicating a magical transformation.

The Mysterious Locket

1. How does the author develop the central idea that looking into the locket's past can help us understand more about Lily's family history?

Answer: B) By showing how the locket and its mysteries are linked to Lily's family story.

Explanation: The story tells us that by learning about the locket, Lily can discover new things about where she comes from and her family's history. It's like a puzzle that connects her to her ancestors.

2. In the story, what does "aura" mean when it says the locket has "intricate engravings and a mysterious aura"?

Answer: C) A special feeling or atmosphere

Explanation: "Aura" in the story means there's something special and mysterious about the locket that you can't see but can feel, like it has its own kind of magic.

3. Why did Lily want to find out all the secrets of the locket?

Answer: B) She wanted to learn more about her family's past.

Explanation: Lily was driven by her curiosity to know more about her own family. The locket was a clue to understanding her family's stories and secrets from long ago.

4. In the story, what does "ancestors" mean when it says Lily was "ready to find out a truth that her ancestors hadn't known for generations"?

Answer: C) Family members from a long time ago

Explanation: "Ancestors" means the people in Lily's family who lived many years before her. They're like branches on her family tree, leading back into the past.

The Mystery of the Whispering Woods

1. Which type of figurative language is used in this phrase?

Answer: C) Personification

Explanation: Personification makes things act like humans. Here, trees 'whisper' and shadows 'dance,' making the woods feel magical and alive

2. Why does the author use this type of figurative language in the story?

Answer: A) To create a vivid and magical setting that captivates the reader.

Explanation: This language makes the woods seem like a magical place you can almost step into, full of wonder and secrets.

3. What motivated Aria to venture into Whispering Woods?

Answer: A) Tales of adventure and the promise of treasure

Explanation: Aria went into the woods hoping for adventure and treasure, inspired by exciting stories.

4. What did Aria realize as she stood before the hidden chamber in the forest?

Answer: A) The importance of friendship and lessons learned

Explanation: Aria learns friendship and the journey's lessons are more valuable than treasure

The Lost Explorer

1. How does Diego's behavior change in the text?

Answer: B) He grows more determined with each obstacle he encounters.

Explanation: As Diego journeys deeper into the jungle and faces various challenges, his determination and courage are tested, but instead of giving up, he becomes more resolute in his quest to uncover the secrets of Eldorado.

2. Select which sentence shows why Diego's feelings changed?

Answer: B) "From treacherous ravines to swarms of biting insects, each challenge brought him one step closer to unlocking the secrets of Eldorado."

Explanation: Every challenge makes Diego more determined to find Eldorado's secrets, showing his growing courage.

3. What is the purpose of Diego's exploration in the narrative?

Answer: C) To uncover the knowledge and adventures that lay ahead.

Explanation: The narrative concludes with Diego's realization that the true treasure of his expedition was not material wealth but the knowledge he gained and the future adventures he anticipated.

4. How does the author develop the central idea that adventure and knowledge are greater treasures than gold and jewels?

Answer: D) By concluding with Diego's realization of what he truly values.

Explanation: Diego realizes true treasures are adventure and knowledge, not gold.

The Magical Forest Picnic

1. What was special about the secret clearing in the forest?

Answer: B) It was enchanted and known only to a few.

Explanation: The passage mentions that the clearing was a secret known only to a select few, indicating its enchanted and exclusive nature.

2. How does the story show that going on a search can lead to exciting new discoveries?

Answer: B) By describing how the friends find a secret clearing for a picnic.

C) By telling about the magical creatures they meet on their adventure.

Explanation: Like finding a hidden playground while exploring, Mia, Jake, and Lily discovered magical creatures and places in the forest, showing that searching can lead to exciting surprises.

3. What does "excitement" mean in the situation where it says "...and hearts full of excitement" as Mia, Jake, and Lily start their adventure?

Answer: C) They were feeling happy and eager.

Explanation: 'Excitement' here means that Mia, Jake, and Lily were filled with joy and eagerness for their adventure, similar to the feeling of anticipation before a fun and new experience.

4. What type of figurative language is used in the phrase "that sparkled like diamonds in the sunlight"?

Answer: B) Simile

Explanation: The phrase uses a simile because it compares the mushrooms' dewdrops to diamonds using the word "like" to show how they sparkle brightly in the sun, just as diamonds would.

The Mystery of Lost Puppy

1. What does "trembling" mean in this context?

Answer: B) Shaking because of feelings, like being nervous or excited

Explanation: "Trembling" here means Emily was both excited and nervous, just like how you feel before doing something big.

2. Choose the text that best describes the story:

Answer: C) Emily finds a lost puppy and decides to help reunite it with its family.

Explanation: The story centers on Emily discovering a puppy that has lost its way. She doesn't just keep the puppy or ignore it; instead, she takes action by searching the neighborhood to find its family. Emily's kind-hearted decision to help the lost puppy find its way back home is what makes this adventure special.

3. How does the story tell us what happened to Emily and the puppy in order, from start to finish?

Answer: C) By telling us each thing that happened, one after the other, until the puppy got home.

Explanation: The story follows a chronological order, which means it tells us what happened step by step. It starts with Emily finding the lost puppy, then shows us how she looks for the puppy's family, and ends with her returning the puppy to them. This helps us understand the story easily, like following a map from the beginning to the end of an adventure.

The Adventures of Captain Courage

1. Which type of figurative language is used in the description "seagulls soared overhead, and ships sailed into the horizon"?

Answer: B) Metaphor

Explanation: The author uses a metaphor to paint a picture of the scene without directly saying "like" or "as." It helps make the port town seem lively and beautiful.

2. Why does the author use this type of figurative language in describing the setting of Seaside Cove?

Answer: C) to highlight its beauty and activity

Explanation: This language makes the port town more vivid and shows it's a busy, pretty place.

3. How does Timmy's view on adventures change by the end of his journey with Captain Courage?

Answer: B) He learns that real adventures are as exciting as he imagined

Explanation: Timmy starts by dreaming of big adventures, and through his journey with Captain Courage, he discovers that real-life adventures are just as thrilling as the ones he imagined. He learns to be brave and the value of experiencing adventures first-hand.

4. What lessons did Timmy learn during his adventures with Captain Courage?

Answer: A) Lessons about bravery, friendship, and the power of imagination.

Explanation: Throughout their adventures, Timmy learns about bravery, friendship, and the power of imagination as they face challenges together, as described in the story.

The Lost Treasure of Pirate Cove

1. How does the story summarize its plot and main theme?

Answer: A) Going on an adventure helps you learn about yourself; it's all about being brave.

Explanation: The story shows how Lily's journey for treasure teaches her about bravery and self-discovery.

2. How does Lily change throughout the story?

Answer: A) She learns to not be afraid, showing she's brave.

Explanation: In her adventure, Lily faces many scary moments but learns to be brave and not let fear stop her. This shows us that even when things get tough, being brave can help us get through anything

3. What does Lily learn during her adventure in Pirate Cove?

Answer: C) Lessons about perseverance and teamwork.

Explanation: Lily learns that being persistent and working with others helps overcome challenges

4. Which sentences should be included in a summary of the passage?

Answer: A) Lily always dreamed of finding the lost treasure of Pirate Cove.

Answer: C) Lily discovers the treasure in a hidden cavern deep within the cliffs.

Explanation: Lily's dream of finding treasure and her discovery in the cliffs summarize her adventure.

The Mysterious Case of Missing Book

1. How does Emily's behavior change in the text?

Answer: A) At first, she is curious but becomes determined by the end.

Explanation: The story starts with Emily being eager and curious about the new library addition and ends with her determinedly solving the mystery of the missing book.

2. Select which sentence shows why Emily changed her feelings:

Answer: D) Initially, she is just interested in reading, but then she discovers a love for adventure.

Explanation: The missing book makes Emily start an adventure. Instead of just reading, she now loves solving mysteries. This shows how she grows and starts to love adventures.

90

3. How is Emily's perspective different from her classmates'?

Answer: A) Emily is focused on solving the mystery, while her classmates are more interested in the book's magic.

Explanation: Emily's friends are amazed by the book's magic, but Emily is more excited about solving the mystery. This shows that Emily and her friends want different things.

4. Which type of figurative language is used when describing Emily's quest as "Armed with her trusty magnifying glass and keen detective skills"?

Answer: B) Metaphor

Explanation: The phrase "Armed with her trusty magnifying glass and keen detective skills" is a fancy way of saying Emily is ready to solve the mystery, like a knight ready for battle. It's not saying she's literally carrying weapons, but it's a way to make her preparation sound cooler and show she's all set to find the book.

ANSWERS TO INFORMATIONAL TEXTS

THE AMAZING WORLD OF DOLPHINS

1. Identify the text structure used in the passage about dolphins.

Answer: D) Descriptive

Explanation: The passage describes dolphins, their behaviors, adaptations, and the challenges they face, fitting best with a descriptive text structure.

2. Cause: Dolphins' ability to use echolocation

Answer: B) They can find food in dark or muddy waters.

3. What is one remarkable adaptation that dolphins have?

Answer: C) They have a strong sense of echolocation

Explanation: Dolphins' remarkable adaptation of echolocation allows them to navigate, locate prey, and communicate effectively in their underwater environment. This ability is crucial for their survival.

4. Select the primary concept that unifies all aspects of the text.

Answer: C) Dolphins are intelligent and adaptive creatures facing various environmental threats

Explanation: The passage shows how dolphins are smart and face challenges, needing our help.

THE MARVELOUS WORLD OF BEES

1. Cause: Bees performing "waggle dances."

Answer: A) Bees are able to communicate precise locations of food and resources.

Explanation: Bees' 'waggle dances' help them tell each other where to find food.

2. Compare the roles within a bee colony based on the passage.

Answer: C) Worker bees maintain the hive, whereas the queen bee's primary role is to lay eggs.

3. What is the main purpose of the passage?

Answer: C) to describe the lives and challenges of bees

Explanation: It's about how bees live, communicate, and face challenges, highlighting why we should protect them.

4. What are some challenges faced by bees mentioned in the passage?

Answer: A) Habitat loss, pesticide use, and climate change

Explanation: Bees face threats like losing their homes, harmful chemicals, changing climates, and sickness.

THE AMAZING WORLD OF RAINFORESTS

1. Select the sentence where the author states opinions:

Answer: D) "Conservation activities are essential for safeguarding and conserving these rich ecosystems for future generations."

Explanation: This sentence says we really need to work on saving rainforests so future kids and animals can enjoy them.

2. Cause: Human activity such as deforestation, agriculture, logging, and mining.

Answer: **Effects:** B) Enhancement of global climate change and biodiversity loss.

Explanation: Activities like cutting down trees harm the climate and lose many plant and animal types.

3. What does "biodiversity" mean?

Answer: C) All the different types of living things like plants, animals, tiny bugs you can barely see, and mushrooms

Explanation: Biodiversity is like a huge nature library with all sorts of living things. Just like books in a library, these plants and animals make our world interesting and help everything work together well.

4. Select the primary concept that unifies all aspects of the text.

Answer: C) Rainforests face significant threats from human activities, necessitating conservation efforts.

Explanation: This part means the story is mostly about how important it is to save rainforests because they are in danger from what people do.

EXPLORING THE SOLAR SYSTEM

1. How does the size and shape of moons compare to the planets they orbit?

Answer: C) Some moons are quite large relative to their planets, while others are tiny and irregularly shaped.

2. What does "cosmic objects" mean in the context of the solar system?

Answer: B) Any natural object outside the Earth's atmosphere, including planets, moons, asteroids, and comets

3. What is the main purpose of the passage?

Answer: C) to introduce the components of the solar system and highlight the importance of exploration

Explanation: The passage introduces us to the solar system's wonders, encouraging us to explore and learn more.

4. What role do moons play in the solar system?

Answer: A) Influencing tides and weather patterns

Explanation: Moons help shape the weather and ocean waves on the planets they circle. Earth's moon makes the ocean tides go in and out, and moons around big planets like Jupiter can make volcanoes erupt and change the weather.

THE AMAZING WORLD OF DINOSAURS

1. Cause: Dinosaurs' adaptations to their environments.

Answer: Effect: A) They dominated the globe for nearly 160 million years.

Answer: Effect: D) they developed features like armor plating, horns, spikes, and feathers.

2. How did herbivorous and carnivorous dinosaurs differ in their lifestyles?

Answer: B) Herbivores ate plants and trees, while carnivores hunted other creatures.

3. What do scientists study to learn about dinosaurs?

Answer: A) Fossils

Explanation: Scientists study fossils, the preserved remains or traces of organisms from the past, to learn about dinosaurs. Fossils provide valuable information about dinosaur behavior, anatomy, and evolutionary history.

4. What is the main purpose of the passage?

Answer: C) To introduce the diversity and significance of dinosaurs and the insights gained from studying them.

Explanation: It's about the diversity of dinosaurs and what we learn from fossils, showing how cool and important they were.

THE MARVELS OF CORAL REEFS

1. Cause: Increasing water temperatures and ocean acidity.

Answer: Effects: C) Coral bleaching happens, and the corals can get sick and might not survive.

Explanation: When the water gets too warm and sour, it hurts the corals, making them lose their colors and become weak.

2. Why coral reefs are called the "rainforests of the sea"?

Answer: C) Because they have lots of different animals and plants living there.

Explanation: Coral reefs have lots of different life (biodiversity), just like rainforests do on land.

3. What roles do coral reefs play in marine ecosystems?

Answer: D) All of the above.

Explanation: Coral reefs provide homes for fish, protect shores, and help people by giving food and jobs.

4. What is the main purpose of the passage?

Answer: C) To tell us why coral reefs are super important and why we need to look after them.

Explanation: The text tells us how important coral reefs are, what dangers they face, and why we should protect them.

EXPLORING VOLCANOES: NATURE'S SPECTACULAR PHENOMENON

1. Cause: The movement of tectonic plates.

Answer: Effects: B) Volcanoes start forming and erupting.

Explanation: When Earth's plates move and bump into each other, it can make the ground crack open and volcanoes to erupt.

2. Which sentence best reflects the author's opinion on the importance of volcanoes?

Answer: B) " Even though they can be scary, volcanoes help change the Earth and are home to many living things."

Explanation: This sentence shows that the author believes volcanoes are not just destructive; they play a crucial role in shaping our planet and supporting life.

3. Select the primary concept that unifies all aspects of the text.

Answer: C) Learning about and watching volcanoes to better understand our planet and keep people safe.

Explanation: The whole text is about how important it is to study volcanoes so we can understand Earth's processes and reduce the risks from eruptions..

4. Why is studying volcanoes important?

Answer: D) For all these reasons: understanding Earth, predicting dangers, and exploring new things.

Explanation: Studying volcanoes helps us grasp how Earth changes, warns us of potential eruptions, and fuels scientific curiosity and discovery.

THE LIFECYCLE OF BUTTERFLIES

1. How is the caterpillar stage different from the chrysalis stage in a butterfly's life?

Answer: A) In the caterpillar stage, it moves around and eats a lot of leaves. In the chrysalis stage, it doesn't move and changes into a butterfly.

2. Select the primary concept that unifies all aspects of the text.

Answer: B) The process of metamorphosis in butterflies.

Explanation: The whole story is about how butterflies change from eggs to beautiful flying insects, a process called metamorphosis.

3. What does "metamorphosis" mean in the context of butterflies?

Answer: B) The change from a caterpillar to a butterfly.

4. What is the primary goal of an adult butterfly?

Answer: B) to find a mate and reproduce

Explanation: The primary goal of an adult butterfly is to find a mate and reproduce. After mating, the female butterfly lays eggs, starting the life cycle anew.

THE IMPORTANCE OF RECYCLING

1. How is using old paper different from making new paper from trees?

Answer: B) Using old paper saves trees and energy, but making new paper uses more.

2. What is the text structure of "The Importance of Recycling" passage?

Answer: C) Problem-solution

Explanation: The passage outlines the problem of waste and pollution, then discusses how recycling serves as a solution to these issues, emphasizing benefits to the environment and economy.

3. What is the main purpose of the passage?

Answer: B) to inform readers about the importance and benefits of recycling.

4. Select the sentence where the author states opinions:

Answer: C) "We can work together to safeguard the earth and create a sustainable future for future generations."

Explanation: This sentence shows the writer thinks everyone needs to work together to take care of the environment and make a better future. It highlights how important it is for all of us to help out.

THE MARVELOUS WORLD OF PENGUINS

1. Compare the swimming ability of penguins to their flying ability.

Answer: B) Penguins are awesome swimmers with their flipper-like wings underwater, but they can't fly.

Explanation: Penguins have adapted to life in the water, with wings that work like flippers to help them swim fast, but these adaptations mean they can't fly in the air like other birds.

2. Select the primary concept that unifies all aspects of the text:

Answer: B) How penguins are built to live in cold places.

Explanation: The whole text talks about the special features penguins have, like thick feathers and sleek bodies, which help them survive and thrive in very cold environments.

3. What are some threats to penguins mentioned in the passage?

Answer: C) Warmer weather, too much fishing, dirty places, and losing their homes.

Explanation: These problems are highlighted as big challenges for penguins, affecting their food supply and living areas, which can make it hard for them to survive.

4. What is the text structure of the passage about penguins?

Answer: D) Descriptive

Explanation: This passage gives us a detailed picture of what penguins are like, how they live, and the problems they face, describing various aspects of their life without following a strict sequence or comparing and contrasting specific elements.

AMAZING ANIMAL ADAPTATIONS

1. How is the way chameleons avoid predators different from how meerkats do it?

Answer: B) Chameleons change color, while meerkats take turns standing guard.

2. Select the Primary Concept:

Answer: B) Animals have special ways to live in their homes.

Explanation: The big idea here is that animals have cool tricks to help them live where they do, like building homes or finding food in hard-to-reach places.

3. How is the story about amazing animal adaptations told?

Answer: D) Describing how different animals live and survive.

Explanation: The story tells us about the awesome ways animals adjust to their homes, like wearing a warm coat in the snow or having night-vision goggles to see in the dark.

4. Cause: Animals adapting to their environments.

Answer: **Effects:** D) All of the above.

Explanation: Animals changing to fit into their homes leads to all sorts of cool outcomes: chameleons blending in, polar bears staying cozy in the cold, and meerkats watching out for each other.

INCREDIBLE INVENTIONS

1. How did the light bulb invention by Thomas Edison compare to earlier forms of lighting?

Answer: B) It gave off more light and was safer and more trusty than candles or oil lamps.

Explanation: Edison's light bulb was a big deal because it made everything brighter without the mess or danger of candles and oil lamps.

2. What's the story mostly about?

Answer: C) How some super smart ideas changed the way we do everyday stuff.

Explanation: The story tells us about amazing gadgets like light bulbs, phones, and smartphones that made our lives easier and more fun. Imagine living without light at night or not being able to call your friend who lives far away. These inventions made all that possible!

3. Which sentence best shows the impact of these inventions?

Answer: B) "These inventions have revolutionized the way we live and interact."

Explanation: These inventions totally changed how we do everyday things, like talking to each other, staying safe at night, and even playing games or doing homework on our phones.

4. Select the Sentence Where the Author States Opinions:

Answer: D) Saying that as we invent more stuff, we're going to see even cooler things

Explanation: Here, the writer is sharing their hope and excitement for the future. He believes that as we get better at making things, we'll see even cooler inventions that we haven't even dreamed of yet!

MARVELS OF THE OCEAN

1. How does the octopus's method of avoiding predators compare to the sea turtle's?

Answer: B) The octopus uses camouflage, while the sea turtle relies on its shell for protection.

Explanation: Octopuses hide by changing color, but sea turtles don't need to because their hard shells keep them safe.

2. What main idea connects everything in the passage?

Answer: B) The cool ways sea creatures live and survive in the ocean.

Explanation: It's all about showing us the cool and different creatures that live in the ocean and what makes them special.

3. Select the sentence where the author states opinions:

Answer: C) "Their extraordinary talents make them one of the most fascinating organisms in the water."

Explanation: Here, the writer is telling us they think the talents of ocean creatures are super interesting, showing us their fascination.

ANSWERS TO MIXED TEXTS

EXPLORING THE ANIMAL KINGDOM

1. Cause: Chameleon's ability to change color.

Answer: **Effects:** A) It can avoid predators more effectively.

Answer: B) It captures prey without being noticed.

2. How do chameleons and octopuses avoid predators?

Answer: B) Each changes its body color, but octopuses can also change their skin texture.

3. What does "camouflage" mean in the context of the animal kingdom?

Answer: C) The capability to blend into the environment to avoid predators or sneak up on prey

4. What is the main idea of the passage?

Answer: b) The unique ways animals adapt to their environments

Explanation: The passage illustrates how different animals, like chameleons, octopuses, and monarch butterflies, have developed unique adaptations to survive and thrive. These include color and texture changes for camouflage, intelligence for solving problems, and long-distance migration to escape seasonal changes.

UNCOVERING MYSTERIES

1. How is the Greek Perspective Different from the Maya?

Answer: A) Greeks focused on philosophy and democracy, while Maya focused on mathematics and astronomy.

Explanation: The Greeks and the Maya were like two different school project teams, each with their own favorite subjects. The Greeks loved discussing ideas and how to live together, while the Maya were experts in math and the stars.

2. Identify text structure:

Answer: D) Descriptive

Explanation: The passage paints a detailed picture of what ancient civilizations did and how they lived, focusing on describing their achievements and lifestyles.

3. Choose the text that best describes the History:

Answer: B) The contributions of ancient civilizations to modern culture.

Explanation: The passage is like a treasure map showing how ancient inventions and ideas, like Greek democracy or Maya calendars, still impact us today.

4. Cause: Studying ancient civilizations.

Answer: D) All of the above.

Explanation: Studying ancient civilizations helps us unlock past secrets—how they built amazing things, lived their daily lives, and came up with smart ideas in math and science, enriching our understanding and appreciation of history.

THE MYSTERY OF LOST KEY

1. Identify text structure:

Answer: B) Sequential

Explanation: The story follows the friends step-by-step on their adventure, like following a path through the woods, showing us each part of their journey in order.

2. Why does the author describe the monsters as "weird"?

Answer: B) to make the story more exciting

Explanation: Describing the monsters as "weird" adds an element of surprise and excitement to the story, engaging the reader's imagination.

3. Select the sentence where the author states opinions:

Answer: C) "The treasure was not the wealth they had discovered but the friendship connections formed."

Explanation: This sentence shares the idea that friendship is more valuable than physical treasures.

4. What is the main purpose of the passage?

Answer: B) To narrate an adventure that strengthens friendship.

Explanation: The story is a narrative focused on the adventure of the friends, highlighting how their journey strengthens their bond.

THE MAGICAL ISLAND ADVENTURE

1. Which type of figurative language is used in the following sentence?

Answer: B) Metaphor, meaning the island was mysterious and full of ancient stories.

Explanation: Saying the island is "cloaked" in fog and stories is a creative way to tell us it's a place full of secrets and adventures, just waiting to be discovered, like a hidden world in your favorite book.

2. How does the text develop the theme that searching can lead to new discoveries?

Answer: D) All of the above.

Explanation: The story shows that being curious and exploring (like a detective on a mission) can lead to awesome finds, from secret places to magical crystals!

3. How does the magical abilities of the island different from the usual places the youngsters have known?

Answer: A) The island has ancient relics and luminous crystals, unlike their usual playgrounds.

Explanation: Imagine finding a playground where the slides glow and there are secret tunnels — that's how different and magical the island is compared to regular places!

4. Select the primary concept that unifies all aspects of the text:

Answer: C) The adventure and discoveries leading to a deeper appreciation of friendship.

Explanation: Everything in the story — from finding the map to exploring the island — shows how going on adventures can make friendships stronger and more special.

THE SECRET OF HAUNTED HOUSE

1. What is the main idea of the passage?

Answer: C) The friends find a treasure instead of ghosts.

Explanation: The story is like a hidden treasure hunt where, instead of encountering spooky ghosts in the "Haunted House," the friends uncover fascinating old treasures and a secret tale about the house's history. It's a delightful twist, akin to expecting a pumpkin but finding a treasure chest!

2. Which type of figurative language is used when describing the "shivers down their spines"?

a) Hyperbole

b) Metaphor

c) Personification

d) Simile

Answer: b) Metaphor

Explanation: The phrase "shivers down their spines" is a metaphor that vividly conveys the friends' fear and anticipation, without them literally turning into ice. It's akin to saying the house's spookiness could make you feel a chilling breeze indoors!

3. Why does the author the figurative language "shivers down their spines"?

Answer: C) to increase the feeling of fear and suspense in the story.

Explanation: This metaphor immerses us into the adventure alongside the friends, making us feel every eerie chill and shadow as though we're right there with them, similar to experiencing goosebumps while watching a horror movie from the safety of your couch!

4. How does the text develop the theme that bravery leads to new discoveries?

Answer: B) The friends decide to explore the house despite their fears.

Explanation: The friends' choice to continue their exploration, despite their fears, illustrates how courage can lead to astonishing discoveries, such as unveiling hidden treasures instead of encountering ghosts. It's like overcoming the fear of the dark to discover there's nothing under the bed after all.

THE MYSTERY OF HIDDEN TREASURE

1. Which text best describes the story?

Answer: B) Young explorers solve riddles to find a hidden treasure.

Explanation: The story is about young explorers who solve puzzles and overcome traps to find a hidden treasure. They learn the value of friendship and adventure along the way.

2. How do the protagonists' behaviors change in the text?

Answer: C) Learn the value of friendship and adventure.

Explanation: Throughout the story, the protagonists learn that the real treasure is the friendship and thrill of adventure they experience together.

3. Select the sentence that shows why the protagonists' feelings changed:

Answer: B) "After solving the last riddle, they realized that the real wealth was the friendship they had built."

Explanation: This sentence shows the change in the protagonists' feelings, shifting from excitement about finding material treasure to realizing that the true value of their adventure lay in the bonds of friendship and shared experiences. It highlights the characters' internal growth and their changed perspective on the meaning of treasure.

4. What does "tenacity" mean in the way it's used in the text?

Answer: C) The determination to overcome challenges and not give up.

Explanation: In the context of the text, "tenacity" refers to the young explorers' determination to overcome obstacles and traps, showing perseverance and not giving up in the face of difficulties.

THE MYSTERY OF MISSING ARTIFACTS

1. Which sentence uses a metaphor or a simile?

Answer: C) "Detective Max entered the dark tunnels like a ship navigating through a stormy sea, with confidence in his heart and resolve in his gaze."

Explanation: This sentence makes a creative comparison using a simile. It likens Detective Max's careful and brave approach to exploring the dark tunnels to how a ship moves through a stormy sea. This comparison helps us picture his courage and the obstacles he faces.

2. What is the meaning of the simile in the chosen sentence?

Answer: C) Detective Max's journey through the tunnels is as challenging and uncertain as navigating a stormy sea.

Explanation: The simile suggests Detective Max's adventure in the tunnels is full of challenges and unknowns, similar to a ship's journey through rough waters. It highlights the difficulty and bravery required in his quest.

3. What does "avarice" mean in the way it's used in the text?

Answer: C) Greed

Explanation: "Avarice" in this story refers to the intense desire for wealth that led Mr. Jenkins, the museum curator, to steal the artifacts. It shows us why he chose to commit the crime.

4. Which two sentences should be included in a summary of the passage?

Answer: B) "To his amazement, the burglar was the museum's curator, Mr. Jenkins."

Answer: D) "Detective Max became triumphant after recovering the treasures and apprehending the offender."

Explanation: These sentences are crucial as they reveal the story's climax and resolution. Mr. Jenkins being the thief is a surprising twist, and Detective Max's success in solving the case and restoring the artifacts brings the story to a satisfying conclusion.

THE SECRET GARDEN

1. What does "mesmerized" mean in the way it's used in the text?

Answer: C) Captivated

Explanation: The term "mesmerized" describes Lucy being completely absorbed and captivated by the fountain's beauty, highlighting the enchanting effect the garden has on her.

2. Which sentence uses a metaphor or a simile?

Answer: C) "The buzzing of bees and birds chirping fills the air, producing a symphony of noises."

Explanation: This sentence uses a metaphor to liken the natural sounds in the garden to a "symphony of noises," creatively comparing these sounds to music without using "like" or "as."

3. What is the meaning of the metaphor in the chosen sentence?

Answer: C) The sounds of nature in the garden are as harmonious and beautiful as a symphony.

Explanation: The metaphor suggests the natural sounds blend as beautifully and harmoniously as a symphony, emphasizing the gardens peaceful and enchanting atmosphere.

4. How does the author develop his purpose of explaining what's special about the garden?

Answer: B) By focusing on Lucy's awe and detailed descriptions of her experiences, the author effectively conveys the garden's magical qualities and its impact on her, inspiring readers' imaginations.

EXPLORING THE MYSTERIOUS CAVE

1. What does "undaunted" mean in the way it's used in the text?

Answer: C) Unafraid

Explanation: In this context, "undaunted" means the friends remained fearless and determined, despite the dangers and challenges they faced in the forest and near the cave.

2. Which two sentences should be included in a summary of the passage?

Answer: A) "According to legend, the cave contained a treasure guarded by a fierce dragon."

Answer: B) "A bold group of friends went on an expedition to discover the cave's mysteries."

Explanation: These sentences highlight the key elements of the story: the legend of the treasure and dragon that motivates the expedition, and the initiation of the adventure by a group of friends.

3. How does the author develop his purpose of explaining what's special about the cave?

Answer: B) Through the friends' daring journey and discoveries inside the cave.

Explanation: The author uses the friends' adventure and the mysteries they uncover inside the cave to reveal what makes the cave special, emphasizing its secrets and the courage it inspires.

4. How does the protagonists' behavior change in the text?

Answer: B) They become more curious and determined as they face challenges.

Explanation: The friends show increasing curiosity and determination as they overcome challenges in the forest and explore the cave's depths, indicating their growing bravery and adventurous spirit.

THE LIBRARY ADVENTURE

1. Which sentence uses a metaphor or a simile?

Answer: B) "Trees murmured secrets in the breeze."

Explanation: This sentence uses a metaphor by suggesting that the trees are capable of murmuring secrets, attributing human-like qualities to them and enhancing the magical atmosphere of the woodland adventure.

2. What does the metaphor "Trees murmured secrets in the breeze" communicate about the magical forest?

Answer: C) The magical forest was alive with mysteries and hidden stories.

Explanation: This metaphor suggests that the forest is not just a collection of trees but a living, breathing entity filled with secrets and stories. It communicates the idea that the magical forest is a place of wonder and enchantment, where every element, even the breeze, is part of the storytelling.

3. How does the behavior of the protagonists change throughout "The Library Adventure"?

Answer: C) Their excitement and curiosity grow as they explore the magical worlds.

Explanation: As the protagonists delve deeper into the adventures offered by the books in the Enchanted Bookshelf, their initial excitement transforms into an even greater sense of curiosity and wonder. This change in behavior highlights the transformative power of reading and the library's magic in igniting the imaginations of its visitors, encouraging them to explore further and immerse themselves in the mystical worlds and ancient civilizations the books reveal.

4. Which two sentences should be included in a summary of the passage?

Answer: A) "This library was no ordinary structure; it was rumored to house volumes that could transport readers to mystical worlds and faraway locations."

Answer: D) "Each successive chapter took them closer to solving the riddles of the past and discovering the secrets of a forgotten civilization."

Explanation: These sentences best encapsulate the essence of the story: the magical ability of the Enchanted Bookshelf and the transformative adventures it offers showcasing both the premise and the climax of their experiences.

Thank you immensely for reaching this point.

Dear Reader,

Our team has invested significant time and effort into crafting this book, aiming to deliver a work of quality and insight.

An opinion from you would not only be incredibly appreciated but also instrumental in helping us share our material with a wider audience.

We are profoundly grateful for your support and sincerely thank you for any feedback you choose to provide!

Made in United States
Orlando, FL
09 December 2024

55269473R00061